THE RAILWAYS OF NORTH LINCOLNSHIRE

C. T. Goode

1985
ISBN 0/9508239/7/X
72 Woodland Drive, Anlaby, Hull. HU10 7HX.

Contents

Abbreviations Used

AJR	Axholme Joint Railway
dmu	Diesel multiple unit
ECML	East Coast Main Line
FO FX	Fridays Only (Excepted)
GCR	Great Central Railway
GDLR	Grimsby District Light Railway
GER	Great Eastern Railway
GG & SJR	Great Grimsby & Sheffield Jc. Railway
GNR	Great Northern Railway
GN of ER	Great North of England Railway
H & BR	Hull & Barnsley Railway
LD & ECR	Lancashire, Derbyshire & East Coast Railway
L & YR	Lancashire & Yorkshire Railway
L & NWR	London & North Western Railway
MR	Midland Railway
MS & LR	Manchester, Sheffield & Lincolnshire Railway
NER	North Eastern Railway
NLLR	North Lindsey Light Railway
SYR	South Yorkshire Railway
SO SX	Saturdays Only (Excepted)
ThO	Thursdays Only
TA & GR	Trent, Ancholme & Grimsby Railway
WR & GR	West Riding & Grimsby Railway
Y & NMR	York & North Midland Railway
XP	Express

Proposed Railways associated with North Lincolnshire. 1821-1913

1821	Cambridge & Lincoln
1827	Cambridge, Lincoln & York
1833	Grand Northern (via Cambridge and Lincoln)
1835	Great Northern (via Cambridge, Sleaford and Lincoln)
1836	Northern & Eastern (via Cambridge, Peterborough and Lincoln)
1837	Hull, Lincoln & Nottingham
1840	Nottingham & Lincoln
1841	London & York (via Cambridge and Lincoln)
1844	Great Northern Boston & Lincoln Loop. Opened 17/10/1848. Closed Woodhall Jc.-Boston 17/6/1963. Lincoln-Woodhall Jc. 5/10/1970 except for odd trips
1844	Swinton, Doncaster & Lincoln. Midland Railway inspired
1844	Sheffield & Bawtry. Bawtry & Gainsborough. GNR inspired
1844	Sheffield & Lincs. Jc. Opened 13/7/1849. Sheffield & Lincs. Ext. to Boston.
1844	Direct Northern. (Peterborough, Grantham, Gainsborough, Snaith, York)
1844	Great Northern.(onetime London & York) Present East Coast route. Opened Retford-Doncaster 1/9/1849. London-Peterborough 7/8/1850. Peterborough-Retford 15/7/1852 (goods), 1/8/1852 (passenger). GN Extension Newark-Lincoln
1844	London & York (Peterborough, Grantham, Gainsborough, Misson, Doncaster)
1844	London & York. GNR. Werrington Jc.-Lincoln opened 17/10/1848. Lincoln-Gainsborough 9/4/1849. Boston-Spalding closed 5/10/1970
1844	Cambridge & Lincoln (via St. Ives and Peterborough)
1844	Eastern Counties. (Above revised)
1844	Lincoln, York & Leeds Direct. (To link above with Y & NM and GN of E at York)(via Gainsborough and Selby)
1844	Ely & Lincoln. Midland Railway inspired)
1844	Eastern Counties. (Ely to Lincoln)
1845	Nottingham & Lincoln. Midland Railway. Opened 4/8/1846
1845	Northampton, Lincoln & Hull Direct
1845	Hull, Great Grimsby & Southampton Direct. (Northampton to Grantham and Lincoln)
1845	Lincoln & Oakham
1845	Lincoln, Leicester & Birmingham Direct
1845	Lincoln & Great Grimsby. (Grimsby, Louth, Horncastle, Lincoln and to Midland line)
1845	Lincs. & Eastern Counties Jc. (Cambridge, Barrow and Hull)
1845	Great Grimsby & Sheffield Jc. (Barnetby-Market Rasen) Opened 18/12/1848
1845	East Coast (Lynn, Spalding, Boston, Lincoln)
1845	Sheffield & Lincs. Jc. Extension (Clarborough-Sykes Jcs.) Opened 7/8/1850. Closed 2/11/1959. Reopened for freight
1845	Lincoln & Retford Jc. Locally promoted line
1845	Retford & Sheffield Jc. Direct
1845	Chesterfield & Lincoln
1845	Lincs. & Eastern Counties Jc. (Hull & Cambridge)
1845	Great Grimsby, Louth, Horncastle & Midland Jc.
1845	Lincoln & Horncastle. GG & SJ inspired
1845	Boston & Lincoln

1845	Eastern Counties. (March-Lincoln)
1845	Spalding & Lincoln
1845	Cambridge & Lincoln Ext.
1845	Lincoln, York & Leeds Jc.
1845	Lincoln & Wath-upon-Dearne. Midland Railway inspired
1845	Eastern Counties Ext. (Lincoln-Milford Jc.)
1845	Direct Northern Revised. Amalgamated with London & York
1845	Peterborough & Boston
1845	Peterborough, Spalding & Boston Jc.
1846	Lincoln & Hull. (Hessle-South Ferriby by roll-on, roll-off ferry, Brigg, Lincoln)
1846	Lincoln, Wainfleet Haven & Boston. Harbour at Gibraltar Point
1846	Saxilby & Clarborough. MS & L. Opened 7/8/1850. Closed 2/11/59. Reopened for oil depot at Torksey, power station at Cottam.
1846	Eastern Counties. (Spalding, Newark, Lincoln)
1847	Stainton, Wragby & Louth. MS & L inspired to block East Lincs. Lincoln Louth line.
1846	Lincoln & Great Grimsby, plus branches to Horncastle and Louth
1847	Tattershall & Horncastle. GNR
1848	Grimsby & New Holland
1848	Barton & New Holland
1854	Horncastle Railway. Opened 11/8/1855. Closed 13/9/1954. Totally 5/9/1971
1862	March & Askern Coal
1863	Spalding & March. GNR. Opened 1/4/1867
1863	Trent, Ancholme & Grimsby. Opened 11/10/1866
1864	Great Eastern Northern. (Long Stanton-Askern)
1864	Gainsborough & Doncaster. GNR. Opened 1/7/1867 (goods), 15/7/1867 (passengers)
1864	Lincoln, Boston, Sleaford & Midland Counties. GNR Honington line. Opened 15/4/1867. Closed 30/10/1965. Lifted 1971
1864	Althorpe & Lincoln
1865	L & Y and GE Joint. (Long Stanton-Barnby Dun)
1865	Spilsby Branch Opened 1/5/1868
1866	Spalding & Lincoln. Joint GN, GE and MS & L venture
1866	Lincoln & Louth. (Five Mile House-Louth)
1869	Firsby & Wainfleet
1871	Coal Owners' Association
1871	Louth & Bardney. Opened 1/12/1876. Closed 5/11/1951. Totally 1/2/1960. Amalgamated with GNR in 1883. Connection at Bardney reversed
1872	Hull, South & West Jc. Tunnel proposed under Humber
1877	Spalding & Lincoln. GNR
1877	Lincoln & Spalding. GER. Mutual blocking
1880	Alford & Sutton Tramway
1880	Brigg & Lincoln Tramway
1883	Hull & Lincoln. (From Hull & Barnsley near Anlaby across Humber on viaduct 7,590ft. long, of 35 spans. Ambitious but rejected due to lack of traffic potential)
1883	Billinghay & Metheringham
1884	Lincoln & Skegness. (Links off MR and GN, then by tunnel beneath city)
1884	Sutton and Willoughby. Opened 14/10/1885
1886	Lincoln, Horncastle, Spilsby & East Coast. (to link two branches)

1887	Chesterfield & Lincoln Direct
1891	Lancashire, Derbyshire & East Coast. (Original intention to tunnel under Lincoln.) Opened Lincoln-Edwinstowe 15/12/1896. Remainder 8/3/1897. Closed to passengers 19/9/1955. Track singled in Lincs. 1971
1898	Lincoln & East Coast & Dock. Revamped LD & ECR
1898	Lincoln, Brigg & Barton-on-Humber. (Foresaw North Lincs. Light)
1898	Trent Valley Light. (Blyton, Scotter, Scunthorpe)
1900	North Lindsey Light
1906	Fockerby & Winterton. L & Y project
1906	Mid. Lincs. Light. (Kirkstead-Sleaford)
1906	Grimsby District
1910	Trent Railway & Bridge. (Fockerby-Whitton)
1910	Barton & Immingham. GCR.
1910	Humber Commercial. (Ulceby-Immingham)
1911	Kirkstead & Little Steeping. GNR. Opened 1/6/1913 (goods), 1/7/1913 (passenger). Closed 5/10/1970
1913	Immingham Tramway. GCR. Closed 9/1961

Although comprehensive, the table does not include all details. Those relevant to lines opened are to be found in the text.

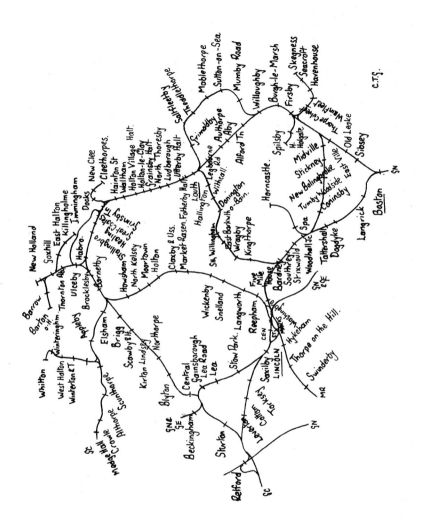

8

Introduction

When I started to set down the history of the railways in North Lincolnshire, I only then realised what a task was before me, as compared with, say, the East Yorkshire area where things were more cut and dried due to the North Eastern Railway monopoly. Here was an attractive, largely flat and unspoilt countryside crying aloud to be criss-crossed by a network of railway lines, much as a freshly painted wall attracts the attentions of the graffiti expert. Some of the less hair-brained schemes materialised; it was realised that no development was likely to take place, and they foundered after lingering on for several decades, leaving in the end a nucleus of two or three main routes geared to freight and holiday traffic. The land remains much as it always was, apart from the heavy industrial developments on the Humber estuary. Places such as Market Rasen have changed little over the years and the railway has made little impression on them. The railway never really did much to serve the village communities, apart from the generous minded Great Northern with its delightful little East Lincolnshire halts; small centres of populace have remained relatively parochial on roads which are left-overs of the pre-war period. Even today the train services make no concession to the new Humber Bridge, for though it is possible to reach Grimsby hourly during a day, a passenger is not encouraged to travel to Lincoln or Gainsborough by rail, for the necessary change at Habrough has never produced decent connections for years, and Habrough is one of the last places in which to dally during most of the year. Scunthorpe is well associated with points to east and west on the railway, and towards the Humber by bus, but connections to the south, including Gainsborough and Lincoln, are surprisingly more typical of the Scottish Highlands than of a county with one part of it set next to the bustling Midlands.

The spirit of the old railways lingers on, best of all perhaps at Barnetby where the station has recently had a welcome cleaning, and its environs. Most charming is the run from there to Lincoln along a line where, at the time of writing, most of the old station buildings and all the signal boxes are still in position, the run taking the traveller through scenery still for the most part unspoilt along the Lincoln Edge.

Currently a local preservation group is attempting to revive the section of line between Grimsby and Louth, including the station at the latter place. Prospects are promising and there is plenty of support for a worthwhile scheme.

I should like to acknowledge the kindly services provided by the Lincolnshire Record Office and Libraries, the House of Lords Library and Public Record Office, Kew; also the Library of the Institute of Civil Engineers. Help has also come from Messrs. B. Longbone, M. Back, L. Franks and the many often anonymous BR staff, past and present, who have answered many questions.

C. Tony Goode.

Anlaby, Hull

The development of Lincolnshire is quite rightly linked with that of the county town of Lincoln, the city strategically placed roughly in the centre of the whole area. The Romans positioned their stronghold on the top of the hill with unsurpassed surveillance of the approaches to the city from all directions, and their own road traffic and that of subsequent generations flowed chiefly between south and north. Across this line of trade flowed the Witham from west to east, and the Fossdyke which conveyed supplies of goods and materials in both directions; wool for export, corn and malt for the West Riding. The canal fell into neglect for some considerable time, however, and road traffic developed alongside it, going to Boston and the banks of the Trent. After 1744 private interests resuscitated affairs, and the canal was given a ruling depth of 3ft.6in. which was satisfactory for all general commerce. The Witham Drainage Act of 1761 improved matters still further, leaving the ultimate difficulty of uniting the two watercourses, Witham and Fossdyke through the High Bridge in Lincoln itself. This was achieved by 1795 and the way was clear for the promising new markets from Lancashire and the Yorkshire woollen towns. Coal and wool were important sources of revenue, and a steady stream of the former came through to the Fossdyke from Derbyshire along the Erewash canal and the Trent. The channel from Lincoln to Boston had been deepened to 6ft. by 1824.

With the roads often in rather a primitive state the waterways were used extensively for passengers as well as freight haulage, and in 1817 two steam packets, 'Witham' and 'Favourite' could be seen plying on the Lincoln-Boston run. A third boat 'Countess of Warwick' appeared in 1818. There was a daily service leaving at 10 a.m., getting to Boston at 4 p.m. Other places were also served, including Gainsborough and Hull once a week. Freight boats on the river to Coningsby, Horncastle and Tattershall also operated to the detriment of markets in these places as trade shifted to the city. At this time London could be reached either via Boston or Hull.

There were mechanical improvements to the vessels after about 1830 which resulted in better services on offer; thus it was possible to cover the Hull-Boston run in one day, travelling by water to Gainsborough, then by road to Lincoln and then back to water for Boston. A day return ticket to Boston from Lincoln cost 15p and to indulge in this one had to set off at 4 a.m. for the six hour run and return twelve hours later.

The Witham Steam Packet Company operated five vessels to Boston, and 'Celerity' was one of the first iron ones. Other sailings could take the traveller to Horncastle, Sleaford, Bardney and Kirkstead. All in all the waterways out of Lincoln were kept fully occupied.

Gainsborough dealt with quite an amount of the Hull and London traffic on behalf of Lincoln and Boston. Ultimately decline set in as the railways came and as roads gained better surfaces. There was a good horse packet service to Horncastle and the growth of stage carriage services arose from about 1832 to Hull, Leicester, Gainsborough and Nottingham, in connection with which a boat left Boston at 7 a.m. to provide a suitable link. An attempt was made to compete with the new transport by putting on a faster boat, the 'Cygnet' with a draught of only one foot, between Lincoln and Boston, but the battle was all but lost and many packet sailings ended in 1860, the canal interests having passed to the Great Northern Railway in 1846. The GNR had put on cheap fares of ½d per mile using 4th Class carriages to compete with the Witham river traffic alongside of which it ran. The Witham lost its traffic first, before the Fossdyke, but some local steam packets lingered on until 1905.

The Trent was of course untouchable and remained as the chief impressive route through the country, running northwards to the Humber to the west of the awakening Frodingham.

To attempt to set out the arrival of the various railways in Lincolnshire in chronological order is tedious and confusing; there were many vague proposals and in any event most of the important ones were in position by 1848. Projected lines were legion, and reference is made where appropriate to the most important of these, while a fuller list appears separately. (P.5)

One way of approaching the subject is to take each interested party in turn, beginning with the Manchester, Sheffield and Lincolnshire Railway Company, itself formed of the Great Grimsby and Sheffield Junction, the Sheffield, Ashton-under-Lyme and Manchester and the Grimsby Docks Company, its offices based in Manchester. An alliance of the above was formed in January 1847, so that early proposals would be made in the names of the constituent companies. Early scheme were grandiose ones, such as the Manchester, Midland, Huddersfield and Great Grimsby Direct from Penistone via Doncaster to Brigg, and the Manchester, Midland and Grimsby Junction from Wortley near Sheffield through Rotherham to Gainsborough. These were nebulous affairs, but the Great Grimsby and Sheffield Junction instituted in September 1844 a survey between Gainsborough and Grimsby with a selection of routes through either Brigg, Market Rasen or Caistor. At the latter place, the least likely to succeed, a meeting was held at the Red Lion, chaired by the local landowner, Lord Yarborough. The Brigg route was chosen and it was also suggested that the town should be linked to Lincoln by a branch to the Midland Railway. The line was opened as far as Market Rasen. Delays ensued due to disputes over the purchase of land and a quarrel with the GNR over running powers into Lincoln from Washingborough. Eventually the line entered the city by way of a limestone cutting at Greetwell. At the north end the original idea had been to enter the branch from the west; in the end the connection was made from the east at Barnetby.

The Gainsborough and Grimsby line was constructed under an Act of 30th June 1845 by John Stephenson & Co., and successfully quashed various other schemes such as the Lincs. and Eastern Counties Junction Railway, the Hull & Gainsborough, Hull & Lincoln Direct Railway and the Isle of Axholme, Gainsborough & Goole.

Further expansion included the extension from Market Rasen to Lincoln, built by Fowler and opened on 18th December 1848 through to the Midland station, the later line of 1863 from Brigg to Cleethorpes and the New Holland-Barton branch. At New Holland the GG & SJR purchased the Humber and Barton ferries for £21,000 as from 26th June 1846 for both passenger and freight use. Three lines were not proceeded with, namely the Gainsborough-Newark which was probably proposed simply to get the Midland to withdraw its own Newark-Gainsborough, a branch to Caistor and a Lincoln-Horncastle line via Stainton towards Louth. To attempt to reach Horncastle and Louth was to bring down the wrath of the GNR whose East Lincolnshire Railway was under construction. So cocksure were the GG &

The first M.S.& L train to enter Grimsby on 28th February, 1848. Reproduced from the illustrated London News, 15th April, 1848. Hull Libraries

SJR that they put down plans for this independent line. However, the GNR refused to yield at a meeting held in London on 4th February 1847 when the GNR was able to strengthen its position regarding the Horncastle branch and also receive an assurance that no line from Lincoln to Louth would be built by anyone else.

On 5th August 1846 an Act was passed for the Sheffield and Lincoln Extension Railway to open a line from Clarborough Jc. east of Retford to Lincoln, entering round the houses by way of Market Rasen. However, commonsense prevailed and a short link was built to the GNR at Sykes Jc. with running powers into the city. This important line was built by Messrs. Peto, Betts and Giles and had a 656yd. tunnel at the Retford end. The GNR could now expand its empire by running traffic reciprocally over the MS & L to Retford and Sheffield. The line cost £80,000; its opening was delayed until June 1850 due to a weak bridge at Torksey and to a dispute between the two companies involved. In December 1949 the MS & L had agreed to compete in alliance with other companies against the GNR for the London traffic. The MS & L would, however, send its traffic over existing routes in exchange for a monopoly to Hull, nor would it touch GNR traffic. The line was opened for goods only in January 1850 with the GNR refusing to let MS & L trains run to Lincoln over the line. Everything was in full swing from 7th August 1850, one reason being that the GNR needed the access to Retford. Still the dispute went on; there was no water for GN engines at Retford, and nasty things happened to GN trains at New Holland. Things were not improved on 19th May 1851 when a GN goods train had an argument with a MS & L passenger train in Clarborough tunnel, for which the unfortunate GNR was to blame.

13

Gainsborough Central Station GCR c.1906   *Collection, C. T. Goode*

The GNR had opened its main line from Maiden Lane to Peterborough in 1850 and was now extending northwards. Originally the plan was to construct a line from Peterborough to Gainsborough running by way of Bawtry and Rossington at the northern end to reach Doncaster which it would pass to the west instead of east as originally intended; local landowners objected to the passage of the line through Rossington, the plan was held up and so there grew the keen interest on the part of the GNR in the Clarborough line to bring traffic to and from Retford and Sheffield. A proposal to route Sheffield trains by way of a branch from Bawtry had already been scotched.

The first section of the easterly flat route of the GNR from Peterborough through Boston and Spalding then on to Lincoln, 58 miles in all was opened on 17th October 1848, two years ahead of the London-Peterborough section. As will be generally known, the early locomotive works for the company were at Boston before their transfer to Doncaster in 1853. The eastern route was the first one operated to the north by the GNR before the opening of the Peterborough Werrington Jc.-Retford line to goods traffic on 15th July 1852 and to passengers a fortnight later. The new station at King's Cross opened on 14th October.

It is remarkable how the pattern of railways in Lincolnshire grew up from small pieces. Up to this time much had been completed, though vital sections remained to be filled. As stated, the GNR had met obstacles north of Retford due to the Rossington worthies; however, work eventually began on the relatively short stretch to Doncaster and the line was opened on 4th September 1849. The route taken had been chosen because of its directness, which brought it to the west of Lincoln and incurred more in the way of adverse gradients.

14

The GNR had to work very hard to get their traffic to anywhere of substance. When the Lincoln-Gainsborough line opened on 9th April 1849 it was found that there was an 'awkward junction' at Gainsborough with the M & SL where GN trains were obliged to reverse in and out of Central station as the inconvenient Lea Road premises had not been completed at the time.

This line was yet another of the jigsaw pieces which in this case was to become part of the Joint line from Doncaster to March and the Eastern Counties.

North of Doncaster at a point just north of the present Shaftholme Jc. the GNR met the Lancashire & Yorkshire branch end-on and could run via Askern along it and over a spur thoughtfully put down by the York & North Midland from Knottingley to Burton Salmon in 1849. This state of affairs existed right up to 1871 when the direct GN line through Selby was opened.

An excellent though uneasy example of early co-operation in joint working was the simultaneous opening on 1st March 1848 of the Grimsby-Louth line of the East Lincs. Company. From the outset proceeds were shared on a 50-50 basis and the MS & L obtained two second hand iron steamers, the 'Queen' and 'Prince of Wales' to operate the ferry service. There were five trains each way daily, with two on Sundays. The GNR would have worked the Louth branch in isolation until the section from Boston was completed. Due to the uneasy relationship between the two companies mentioned above, the GN workings to New Holland ceased on 1st September 1851.

Louth Sta. c1968   *C. T. Goode*

The MS & L was a fast mover once it had started creating its empire. On its New Holland line the stations at Goxhill, Ulceby, Habrough, Stallingborough and Great Coates were opened from the outset, with Thornton Curtis a little later some half a mile nearer to Ulceby than the final version at Thornton Abbey. Thereafter followed the opening of the line to Market Rasen on 1st November 1848, with stations at Brockelby, Barnetby, Moortown, Holton and Usselby, with the extension to Lincoln opening on 18th December with the two stations at Wickenby and Langworth. The later stations at Howsham, Snelland, North Kelsey and Reepham were opened in February 1849.

GCR Steam rail motor on Hull-Barton Service   *Collection, C. T. Goode*

The little branch from New Holland to Barton opened on 1st March 1849 without the diminutive halt at Barrow Haven which, however, soon followed on 8th April 1850. The initial service on this line was generous, with six weekday and two Sunday trains down and five weekday and three Sunday trains up.

On 2nd April 1849 the Brigg-Gainsborough opened, together with its stations at Scawby & Hibaldstow, Kirton Lindsey, Northorpe and Blyton. Initially, due to the lack of the link between Brocklesby and Habrough, passengers for Grimsby had to change at Ulceby to and from New Holland trains. This vital piece of the jigsaw was put in when the line was opened throughout from Sheffield to Retford by completion of the Woodhouse Jc.

(Sheffield)-Gainsborough portion on 16th July 1849. This was of course the route the GN took when exercising running powers via Sykes Jc. and Clarborough Jc. The Trent Bridge at Gainsborough was designed by John Fowler and comprised two spans with plate girders each 154ft. long. The total length was 460ft. on three piers, one of which rested in the river. Work began on 4th May 1848 and there was some difficulty in rolling the girders into place because of the nature of the river. This was finally done up the approach embankments and the structure was opened on 11th July 1849.

With the opening of the GN direct route Lincoln's prime position diminished, and the Loop line became a subsidiary line and one used for excursion traffic. The direct route had only relatively light traffic in the early days with but one fast train serving Leeds and taking 5½ hours. The run from London-York via Askern took five hours but had the merit of being quicker than anything anyone else could offer.

The third entrant into Lincoln was the Midland Railway, and before this movement is recorded, more of the background machinations should be considered. Lincoln was an attractive prize to aspiring promoters approaching from the south. The town was growing and prosperous with a population of 14,000; the going was easy, but whether one headed for Boston or Grantham, the two most promising places, the transit was through sparsely populated areas much as today. As noted, the GN laid down a firm line of route northwards with its East Lincolnshire route towards Louth. Prior to this successful proposal there had been two earlier ones which had stimulated MR interests in Lincolnshire. The first was the Grand Northern Railway of 1823, proposed by Cundy and of 182 miles to take in Lincoln on the way to York. The other was Gibb's line of 1835 on a similar line of route and entitled the Great Northern Railway, the name having nothing to do with the genuine article of 1845.

Also on the table in the game of getting to York was the Y & NM (later MR) route of 220 miles and with 12 tunnels. Of the first two proposals Cundy's route was chosen, and this was dismissed by the House of Commons who favoured the lengthier Y & NM route which was opened in 1840 and brought Derby and Nottingham into the picture.

The Y & NM had had designs on Lincolnshire and East Anglia right from the outset, and had looked with interest at what the Northern and Eastern Railway Company were planning further south. Lincoln Council had encouraged their scheme of 1836, basically the same as Cundy's, from London to Cambridge, then on to Lincoln and York with a branch to Norwich. This was not pursued further, though it came up again in 1844 in Walker's Cambridge & York Railway which was to link up with the Y & NMR. Other schemes were put forward, including one by the Earl Fitzwilliam, but eventually they all settled to a recognisable pattern helped by the Cambridge-York sponsors combining with the GNR faction. This was co-ordinated into the East Coast Main Line as today, but with a run through Gainsborough instead of Retford and surveyed by J. Walker as the London & York Railway. To summarise the developments from the south:- J. Walker's line was known as the Fens line and ran east of the hills to Lincoln. This line was modified in form by Walker's successor Joseph Locke and then furthered by Cubitt, who suggested amalgamation with the London & York scheme, Gibb's Towns line.

As far as Lincoln itself was concerned, the first rail connection was set on 16th April 1838 when the 'Railway' coach left there at 6 a.m. to run via

Lincoln High St. crossing. The GN station is seen in the background.   *C. T. Goode*

Sleaford and Northampton and reach Denbigh Hall on the London & Birmingham Railway, later the London & North Western. From there a train reached London at 9 p.m. The return journey was at 7.30 a.m., giving an arrival in Lincoln at 10 p.m. By the following year things were a little easier when a coach left Lincoln at 9.30 a.m. to meet a train at Wansford on the Northampton-Peterborough branch. Now the arrival in London was 8.30 p.m.; the return left at 10.45 a.m. and the coach reached Lincoln at 9 p.m. All this compared will with the boat journey which might well take up to 38 hours but was still used by some 36,000 passengers yearly.

The MR station at Lincoln St. Marks, now closed to traffic.   *C. T. Goode*

Later the LNWR were to make use of the running powers acquired by the favour bestowed by running to Lincoln and even to New Holland. The through service began in February 1856, involved the MS & L and MR and was a train calling at Rugby from Euston, then Lincoln, Market Rasen and Barnetby. The intriguing service was only in operation for a short period.

The MR branch at Lincoln came about as a result of the speculation common at the time, with would-be entrepeneurs in the Midlands placing a ruler on the map and visualising an outlet for their products on the Humber where the ports were most convenient for the European markets. On this ruled line fell Lincoln, strategically placed as always, and Newark, a growing town which was one of the prime centres of malting in the United Kingdom.

A welter of proposals was heard, the most sonorous being the Hull, Lincoln & Nottingham Railway of 1837, sponsored in Lincoln and with designs on Bristol. The L & YR put down a proposal labelled the Northampton, Lincoln & Hull Railway, which was to reach Lincoln from the east from Grantham, trains reversing on to an extension to the GG & SJR line at Market Rasen. This was evidently not a serious proposition as it was used to attempt to thwart the MR who had put up a Lincolnshire Junction Railway running in theory from Swinton, then Doncaster to Gainsborough. Several of the would-be projects, as the last named, missed Newark altogether; of these the MR Extension was adopted and was opened from Nottingham on 3rd August 1846. The station in Lincoln, later St. Marks was built by a local contractor, John Burton. The engineer for the line was Barlow. Refreshment facilities were added to the station at the west end in 1849 and the complement of staff at the site was 37. Possibly the station at Newark, later Castle was designed by the same architect I. A. Davies who also produced the Tudor masterpiece at Thurgarton. The station was of Yorkshire stone and was busy from the outset with both passengers and a heavy cattle traffic.

The GNR Loop line entered Lincoln a little after the MR. In 1848, their premises being just down the High Street. Then, on 18th December 1848 the MS & L arrived from Market Rasen, forming a junction with the GNR at Durham Ox Jc. and running to the eastern platform ends of the MR station just over the level crossing, a complicated arrangement which was to exist for many years.

The Great Eastern Railway were seeking an outlet to the north and a portion of the lucrative coalfields in Yorkshire, Nottinghamshire and Derbyshire. This they hoped to do by working arrangements with other companies, principally the GNR whom they could see successfully expanding in all the right directions. Southern interests had been active before this, producing the expected sorts of schemes, First came the March & Askern Coal Railway, planned from Crowland, by-passing Spalding and passing through Lincoln on a viaduct 1,650 yards long with a swing bridge over the Trent at Torksey giving two 40ft. openings. This was opposed because of the lack of concern for the amenities in Lincoln and the uselessness of the project to landowners on the way. There would have been off shoots to Sheffield and Grimsby.

The Great Eastern Northern Junction Railway had been vying with the GNR to secure the route from Gainsborough to Doncaster, this being part of a bold attempt to seek coal traffic by promoting a coal only line. This would have no gradient of more than 1 in 400, an easy achievement in view of the terrain from Long Stanton (Cambridgeshire), through Lincoln, Blyton, Haxey and ultimately to Askern where there were collieries and the ever waiting L & YR. The whole line would be engineered by Fowler and Hawkshaw and would be 108 miles long. The L & Y also wished to enter the act and floated a similar scheme of their own, this 113 miles long from Askern to Long Stanton and to be built with the connivance of the GER who would allow the L & Y to reach Liverpool St. This and the other scheme were defeated in Parliament on 14th March 1865; possibly at a cost of £12,000 per mile the latter project was a little too daunting. It was also to be passenger carrying line with the thinly disguised purpose of blocking GNR interests in the West Riding.

The relationship between the GE and GN was an uneasy one and very much a marriage of convenience. By a Bill of 1863 the GE wished to extend its route from March to Spalding and asked for running powers over the GN from March to Doncaster. The GN were unhappy and put forward a counter proposal for their own line from Spalding to March which was accepted on condition that the GE would be allowed running powers. The GN also wished to push ahead with the completion of the Loop line from Gainsborough to Doncaster instead of using the unsatisfactory Retford route via Sykes Jc. and the MS & L who, it will be recalled were not exactly cordial. Nor were the GNR keen on GER incursions northwards, so sought to offer running powers for their mineral trains only between Spalding and Doncaster. However, the GER wanted more than this, having an eye on the South Yorkshire coal, almost all of which was off to London via the MS & L at Doncaster and the GNR. They thus demanded joint ownership of the embryo Gainsborough-Spalding line and also that section between Spalding and March. The GNR agreed and the necessary powers were obtained.

During 1867 two sections were completed, one of which was the coveted Doncaster-Gainsborough line on 15th July, while the other was that from March to Spalding on 1st April.

At this time the GN and GE had been involved in a non-starter, the Goole, Keadby and Haxey Railway of 1865, in which the L & Y and MS & L would have made an uneasy foursome. The L & Y appear to have been the prime movers in the line which would have crossed the MS & L near the remote Godknow Bridge in the north west corner of the country.

In Gainsborough a second station at Lea Road appeared to save the earlier reversals into the MS & L premises. This was situated well out of the town and in July 1867 the townsfolk demanded a shuttle service between the two stations without any success. This could have been a useful idea, workable even without the triangular junction which had been proposed here in 1864 without result, though the land existed. The GNR crossed the Trent using the MS & L bridge, performing engineering contortions to get round from each bank.

So far, so good. Things were reasonably cordial and all set for a line to be laid between Lincoln and Spalding. This was held in abeyance until later, in 1876 as the GER was in a parlous financial state, with the result that the GNR had to revert to moving its mineral traffic over the MS & L and exploiting its own main line via the Nottingham-Grantham branch opened in 1863. So unstable were GER fortunes at this time that amalgamation was considered with the GN. No doubt thoughts of this kind caused the patient to recover quickly and to consider the next suggestion by the GN that all the lines

20

owned by the two companies between Cambridge and Doncaster should be jointly owned and projected with running powers granted to the GNR from Huntingdon to Cambridge and Ely to Yarmouth. Weak the GER might have been, but not too weak to sense a possible takeover, and so turned down the ideas.

In 1878 the GER took down from the shelf and dusted the 1864 scheme for a line to Askern from Sleaford, linking up with the L & YR coal. the GNR threw in a counter proposal for a more modest line to Lincoln from Sleaford, withdrawing the proposals for running powers to the East Anglian coast and suggesting that the Joint line should begin at Huntingdon. This proposal was accepted on condition that the rather downtrodden GER were given running powers to Doncaster which was, after all, not so far from Askern and within tapping range of the MS & L coal.

By an Act of 1879 there thus came into being a Joint Line running through from Black Carr Jc. (Doncaster) through Gainsborough, Lincoln, Sleaford, Spalding, March and St. Ives to Huntingdon, to be administered by a Committee made up of five Directors of the GNR and GER respectively.

With the Gainsborough-Lincoln section already finished, followed by the detached run from March to Spalding and the Doncaster-Gainsborough section, the remaining pieces of the jigsaw were completed as follows: Spalding-Ruskington 8th March 1882 and Ruskington-Pyewipe Jc. 1st August 1882. Apart from a point of contact east of Lincoln at Greetwell Jc. with the GN proper, the Joint Line pursued its own independent way south of the city to Pyewipe Jc. on the north east side where sidings and the old Gainsborough line were encountered. The GER shed was at Pyewipe Jc. Lincoln was the Headquarters of the line, with its own Manager at High Street station, an eventual refuge of four companies, the GN, GC, GE and LD & ECR, leaving the MR as the rather stand-offish sole occupant of its own premises near St. Mark's church. Each of the two joint companies provided its own trains and crews, and GN line maintenance was delineated north of Sleaford. The revenue was perhaps disappointing, especially to the GN who lost out through reduction of goods handling at centres such as Peterborough, March and Huntingdon. Much of the revenue came from through traffic and not a great deal was generated from the roadside.

As well as Lincoln, Sleaford had an avoiding line provided for it, and it must be stated that not the whole of the line was purely joint, there being running powers for the GER through Spalding and for the final three miles or so over the GNR into Doncaster. The GN enjoyed similar privileges through the station area of March.

Both had running powers only over the vital Trent bridge at Gainsborough, built by the MS & L. The ruling gradient of 1 in 400 was adhered to, with a level stretch near March. Two runs of 1 in 200 faced trains near Stow Park and Blankney; there were also some tight curves here and there.

To the east of the Trent was the vast ironstone countryside around Frodingham which had hitherto been unexploited. Agriculturally the land was not distinguished and had only provided good rough shooting for the local landowner. The son of one of them, Rowland Winn had, however, shown interest in the new technology and had, in November 1859, constructed a short length of railway to the bank of the Ancholme river at Thornholme. He encouraged his two brothers Henry and William, and George Dawes to let out the beds of ironstone which they owned and allow the stone to be carted to wharves on the river to be shipped to South Yorkshire for processing. Dawes had already set up the first furnace on the Ancholme and it was now clear that a railway would be useful, so in October 1859 it was decided to lay down a line from the ore pits to the east of Frodingham to the original piece of track built by the Ancholme, for which Dawes would provide the labour and materials, while Winn would provide timber and of course the right of way. By an Agreement of March 1860 the line was completed, but Dawes was not satisfied, considering that the Trent was a better river on which to base his transport and so proposed a line through the hill from east to west and so out on to the plain.

The South Yorkshire Railway who had arrived from the west and was on the wrong side of the river, were naturally very interested, especially as they had had something similar in mind which, however, contrived to miss the ironstone and pass directly south east towards Brigg. The MS & L, however, of which the SYR was a constituent, had a scheme of their own which was nearer the mark, running from Barnetby to Keadby. Heat was therefore generated between the two factions, and while they smouldered the Trent, Ancholme & Grimsby Railway, as Winn's concern was called, got on with matters, formed on 22nd July 1861 to put down a line from Frodingham to Barnetby with authorisation for the works already mentioned. They had capital of £120,000 and shares were held by three main parties, Dawes/Winn, the SYR and MS & L, both of whom had managed to get in on the act, with desirable running powers. The SYR also obtained the necessary Act to cross the Trent from Althorpe over a waterway which was 475ft. wide at this point, full of barges with high rigging, so that there was a constant outcry from aggrieved boatmen about the likely dangers to navigation caused by anything that might be erected across their path. The contract was awarded to Fairburn & Sons of Manchester for £20,000 and in January 1862 work on the west bank began. There was a line of 6ft. diameter tubes sunk 55ft. deep as a foundation; there were five spans along the length of 484ft. with a swing span of 160ft. which gave a clearance of 27ft. when opened, to the railway above the mean depth of water of 18ft. at low tide. The width of the bridge was 25ft. and this included the sensible provision of a footpath.

Tests were made on 1st July 1864 and the first engine across was No. 4 'Wharncliffe' with Driver Woodley on loan to the SYR from the MS & L. The Inspector failed the structure and suggested that the swing span should be increased to give an opening of 200ft. off centre at the fourth span. Eventually the bridge opened to freight first, then to passengers along with the whole 14 mile stretch from Gunness Jc. to Wrawby Jc. on 1st October 1865.

Originally there were stations at Althorpe, Frodingham, Appleby and Elsham which were not overstretched by the two trains each way on weekdays only. Trains left Frodingham for Doncaster at 10.26 a.m. and 4.07 p.m. and for Grimsby at 10.39 a.m. and 6.09 p.m., with a 9.12 a.m. train to New Holland on Tues, and Fri. only. Of Frodingham more later; its growth was phenomenal and the first station was east of the Brigg road level crossing and replaced in 1887. On the river bank the Keadby terminus was closed on 1st November 1874, while Althorpe which had opened on 2nd August 1869 then became Keadby & Althorpe. There were no Sunday trains until July 1892.

Running up to Frodingham was the Scotter road viaduct of 1,020yd. in length taking the line along at 80ft. on 85 30ft. arches. This was built by Verity of Doncaster. Frodingham was entered by a cutting 70ft. deep.

The import of coal across the Trent and outlet for the iron ore helped immensely in developing the process of smelting, and in the early years of the line some ten furnaces were brought into service by six firms away from the river bank. In 1873 the Santon branch was opened to serve the ironstone activities on Lord Yarborough's estates.

The TA & GR engines were from frustrated exports, bought from Beyer, Peacock for £2,675 each and intended for the Sardinian Railways. They became MS & L Nos. 212-5, the Class 15s and began life in green with red, white and black lining. As far as it is known the company had no rolling stock. With the linking up of Grimsby exports boomed and the traffic flow moved in the wrong direction for the health of the TA & GR. The MS & L had taken over the SYR on 16th July 1874 and the TA & GR lost its nominal independence on 12th July 1882.

The route of the TA & GR later became more important than could ever have been envisaged by its promoters, once the West Riding and Grimsby line, a joint GNR and MS & L affair, had joined the old SYR at Stainforth Jc., thus opening up directly the whole of the West Riding with its great potential, and after the short but vital spur to the Doncaster-York section of the East Coast Main line had been put in to join the WR & G at Applehurst Jc.

Grimsby virtually began from nothing, having humble commercial origins in the Grimsby Haven Company of 1799 set up to administer a fishing business. At that time there was a settlement of 1,000 or so. In 1846 the MS & L purchased the above company and set about its development. Basic commodities handled at the port, apart from fish, were timber, pit props, wood pulp for a local paper mill and the export of coal, chiefly from the Midlands. In its final basic form during its heyday there were three docks covering about 500 acres of land and 140 acres of water. For those who like statistics, there were 81 miles of railway serving six miles of quayside. Dominating the scene was the hydraulic tower of 306ft. looking as if set up to call the dockers to prayer each morning. In 1864 the MS & L took over the passenger vessels operating out of Goole and serving all the notable ports in near Europe. The GNR had a large warehouse in the Fish Dock to which it had running powers.

Between 1866-72 the contractors Logan & Hemingway were involved in various improvement works in the Grimsby area. A new customs house was opened in February 1875, while on the west side of the Old and Royal Docks new coal booths were installed for which the two mile Great Coates branch was opened on 2nd March 1879. On 22nd June 1879 the Prince of Wales opened the Union Dock, while the Alexandra Dock was available for use in July 1880.

Land at £150 per acre tempted plans for a new dock at Killingholme in 1874. Unfortunately such a scheme was not proceeded with. Further north,

Cleethorpes original station. C. T. Goode

of course, the port of Immingham was developed, built to cope with the increase in the coal and timber trade at the turn of the century and opened on 22nd July 1912, though partially in use one week earlier. This allowed Grimsby further to develop its role as prime fishing port.

Cleethorpes signalbox. Roller Coaster in the background. C. T. Goode

Cleethorpes was the 'fun' part of the area, in contrast to the working area of Grimsby, and like so many other places owed its existence to the railway. In 1872 a 1,200ft. pier was opened by the Cleethorpes Pier Company in this very quiet spot served by a single line from Grimsby. When it was realised what was in the offing, the Company astutely doubled it on 25th May 1874 and opened New Clee station on 1st July 1875. Seeing the interest shown by the railway, they were asked by the Urban Sanitary Authority to preserve the cliff front 'for recreational purposes'. The line was extended along the front, a most exciting approach for the small boy, right to the pier entrance itself, and money was set aside to the tune of £33,000 for the sea defences alone. The MS & L went into the entertainment business in a really big way, with £10,000 invested in public baths, a colonade, refreshment rooms and stalls, plus a grotto, pier pavilion and gardens. Later the railway was to buy all the foreshore between Grimsby and Cleethorpes in 1892 for £4,500. The investments paid off and up to 30,000 people were known to visit the resort on a single day, causing some jealousy on the other coast at Blackpool. In 1909 the terminal station at Cleethorpes was modernised and given a different layout which was not as good as the original. One interesting and often puzzling fact was the apparent lack of locomotive facilities in obvious places like Grimsby Town station and Cleethorpes, where there was a turntable. After the opening of Immingham shed in 1913 engines would make the trip to and from there, while prior to this there was a small depot on the south side of the lines at Grimsby Docks station.

To take the developments at Immingham in more detail:- Following the unproductive suggestion for a dock at Killingholme in 1874, nothing was done until 1900 when the Commercial Dock Company proposed something similar. The GCR was willing to lend support, provided that the people of Grimsby were also willing to show interest, though it was clear that they favoured Immingham as a site and bought land from the Earl of Yarborough. Fears were expressed locally that the Immingham site would be a bad one, due to silting, but surveys were carried out and satisfaction was expressed, with the result that the Humber Commercial Railway & Dock Act of 1901 was formulated, set out more specifically in a second Act of 1904. The first sod was cut on 12th July 1906 and special trains conveyed guests to the ceremony from Marylebone, Manchester, Chester and Cleethorpes, all the trains using the contractor's line from Grimsby.

The opening was a splendid affair, performed by the King and Queen on 22nd July 1912 before 1,400 guests in one of the Transit sheds. Music was supplied by the Cleethorpes Pier Orchestra. Their Majesties were brought to Grimsby Docks station, then to Immingham by the 'Atlantic' engine 'Lady Henderson'. More special trains came from London and other places en route, and speeches were heard in another Transit shed, where also the General Manager of the GCR. Sam Fay, was knighted.

The East Lincolnshire Railway was authorised in 1846, opened in sections and was ready for use in 1848. Its run of 78 miles from Peterborough was the only line east of the Lincolnshire Wolds from Caistor to Horncastle, and with the linking up of Grimsby and Lincoln with Louth and Boston it was hoped that development would result. In actual fact most places stayed much as they had been and it was local enterprise which produced the short branch lines off the main line and the resultant flow of holiday traffic from the west to the newly established seaside resorts which caused any great changes in the undisturbed rural tranquillity. It will be remembered that the GNR had inaugurated with the MS & L a joint service between Louth and New Holland on 1st March 1848. Louth had been quite a busy market town before the railway came, full of red brick houses and with its remarkable church of St. James boasting a nave 182ft. long and a spire 294ft. high. Cattle had always been the main business in Louth, and the market there dated from 1551 in the reign of Edward VI. Dealers would come here from as far afield as Manchester, Nottingham and Birmingham, and the railway soon took its share of the traffic with stock worked in and out on early passenger trains. Friday was the main day for activity and the loading docks were normally busy between 11 a.m. and 6 p.m. on that day when specials ran to meet the fish workings out of Grimsby and the goods from Boston. Louth will be seen to have been a magnet for other railway schemes besides the East Lincolnshire, a successful one of which the GNR fully realised the potential and leased it at a handsome £36,000 per annum.

To take the small local branches as they developed. Spilsby was a small town of 1,500 inhabitants which thought itself worthy of a rail connection, so that a branch was authorised on 5th July 1865 and opened along its four mile length on 1st May 1868. There was intermediate station at Holton Holgate. Things went fairly steadily for many years, but it was obvious that the GNR had backed a loser. However, the passenger train service survived until the beginning of the Second World War.

The line from Boston to Lincoln had managed to miss Horncastle, which lay to the north. In 1846 the GNR had proposed a branch from Tattershall to Horncastle which was, however, rejected in 1847. In 1854 the Horncastle Railway Company was formed to lay down a branch from the main line at Kirkstead. This run of 7½ miles was opened on 11th August 1855 and was of course worked by the GNR as their own branch, being nominally independent until 1923. The engineer was Cubitt and contractor Thomas Brassey. An interesting place on the branch was Woodhall Spa, situated some 1½ miles off the main line and more easily identified once Kirkstead became known as Woodhall Jc. This was a small health spa where iodine and bromine were discovered as a sideline to mining prospecting. The resort was served by the only intermediate station, apart from the somewhat distant junction. Trains could run directly on to the branch from the Boston direction, though branch trains from Woodhall Jc. had to run east for a short way, then reverse to gain the single line, which enjoyed a profitable and happy life.

Louth was joined to Lincoln across the Wolds by a pleasant and scenic line from Bardney, again on the main line from Boston. This was promoted by the Louth & Lincoln Railway of 1866 which took its course via Wragby from Bardney. Work began in September 1871 but the going was physically and financially rough. However, the line opened to goods traffic on 26th June 1876, and to passenger trains in December of that year. So near bankruptcy was the line that the usual celebrations were dispensed with. The GNR had agreed to operate the trains in return for a half of the revenue; however, under the Act of 10th August 1882 the GNR took control and the amalgamation was rendered official on 30th June 1883. The connection with the main line was at first similar to that at nearby Woodhall in the case of the Horncastle line. A triangular layout was then suggested, but finally the line came in from the western end of the layout. The length of the Bardney-Louth line was 22 miles and was single, apart from the necessary passing places. The maximum

J11 on branch train at Horncastle   *Collection, C. T. Goode*

gradient was 1 in 70 and tunnels were made, at Withcall and South Willington. The line was too expensive to be successful, and though it did cut off a corner, it never attracted more than four or five trains per day.

Yet another line was connected with Louth, namely the Mablethorpe Loop which took in the little resort in a coastal sweep of 23 miles, compared with the direct run of 13 miles between Louth where the line left, and Willoughby where it rejoined. The first part of the route opened was the 12 miles from Mablethorpe Jc. south of Louth to the resort itself, on 17th October 1877, this under the cognomen of the Louth & East Coast Railway Company authorised on 18th July 1872. The Act also included a branch from Saltfleetby station to the Haven and an extension to North Somercotes, though these were not needed after the course of the main line had been eased to accommodate the places in question. Nothing ever being as obvious as it looks, the next section opened was the Sutton-on-Sea & Willoughby Railway of 28th July 1884, in action from 14th October 1885 which left the gap between the two small towns, they numbered 5,300 together in 1958, to be completed by a three mile link opened on 14th July 1888. The whole line was single with passing loops and was worked by the GNR throughout.

Mablethorpe and Sutton-on-Sea were but pale creatures compared with Skegness, a small place on the coast further south which had a phenomenal growth from 1,488 originally to something approaching 13,000 in 1958. Both the 9th Earl of Scarbrough. who owned estates in the area, and John Hassell's 'Jolly Fisherman' advertisement for the GNR helped to foster this growth. Originally Skegness was linked to rail by a horse bus to and from the

27

C12 on Bardney branch. GN signals prominent. M. Black

nearest station on the line, at Burgh-le-Marsh. The first projection of a line towards the town was embodied in the Firsby & Wainfleet Railway, authorised on 13th May 1869 running over the formation of the latterday north curve at Firsby from the station on the main line. The south curve was the important one for the excursion traffic; this was put in during 1881. An intermediate station served Thorpe Culvert, while Wainfleet itself was at the time a small market town of 1,500 and the GNR had agreed to operate the line and convey the plentiful agricultural produce for 60% of the revenue.

It was not long before the Wainfleet & Firsby Extension Railway was mooted, authorised on 18th July 1872 and opened to Skegness on 28th July 1873, leaving Wainfleet by a rather sharp curve. There were two stops en route, at Croftbank and Cowbank, later Havenhouse and Seacroft. The line was originally single, but was doubled about 1900. The normal passenger service was from 6-10 trains each way daily.

Excursion traffic developed very nicely for the GNR via the new lines to both Skegness and Mablethorpe. However, there was one fly in the ointment in that workings from Lincoln had to travel by way of Boston to gain the East Lincs line; if they had gone via Bardney and Louth they would have had to reverse twice! What was needed, therefore, was a cut-off to bring these trains into the right running direction, that is, towards Firsby and missing Boston, and so the Kirkstead & Little Steeping Railway was authorised, opening for goods on 1st June 1913 and to passengers one month later. There were five stations on the comparitively short line, including the charmingly named Tumby Woodside. Thus, Woodhall Jc. gained another branch line of importance, leaving the main route at Coninsby Jc. and joining the East Lincs. Railway at Bellwater Jc.

Earlier promoters had foreseen troubles with the routing of Midlands holiday traffic to the Lincolnshire coast, and had put forward at least two schemes to expedite matters. The Lincoln & Skegness Railway of 1884 would have run directly, with connections to companies on the west side of Lincoln, north and east passing beneath the city in a tunnel 1,280yd. long, running to Horncastle and arriving in Skegness near the Vine Hotel on the road to Gibraltar Point. Nothing came of this plan.

The history would be much larger if all the whimsical schemes were chronicled in detail and these, many of which were very tentative, would simply overshadow the lines which did in fact materialise. The Mablethorpe

Woodhall Jc. Note elaborate nameboard and iron urinal.   *H. C. Casserley*

Firsby GNR, North end.   *H. C. Casserley*

area had its share of such schemes, and two are worth detailing for their unusual nature. Getting to the coast from the main line was the chief need, and prior to the loop line came quite sensible suggestions for direct routes. Alford was a small town due west of Mablethorpe, and it was expected that a company would, sooner or later put down a line running east. First in the field was a proposal of 1873 which foundered due to the hints of the Willoughby-Sutton project in the air. However, it was decided to try a narrow gauge system, using the new steam tram locomotives which were in vogue at the time, and two proposals were set out, the first being that for a 2ft.6in. line from Alford to Sutton-le-Marsh, and a second called the Skegness, Chapel St. Leonard and Alford Tramway which was intended to run into the main line, rather ambitious in view of the gauge difficulty. The latter was shelved after 1885, leaving the first to open on 2nd April 1884.

While reviewing the early narrow gauge attempts in North Lincs., mention should be made here of an ambitious little scheme to strike such a line northwards from Lincoln to Brigg. This was the Lincoln & Brigg Tramway of 1880 which was to be of 3ft.6in. gauge and 23 miles in length. The surveyors were Goddard & Son of Lincoln and the engineer A. Skill of Grimsby. A start was made at the Brigg end and in fact six miles of track were laid by 1888; however, the total cost was £90,000 and support was not readily available. The route was to run down the centre of roads, crossing the MS & L on the level at Scawby and going by way of Hibaldstow and Redbourne, Caenby Corner and on to Lincoln. The terminus there would have been useful for the cartage of passengers and freight, particularly over the hilly parts of Lincoln. However, the lack of support and pressure from railway interests killed the scheme and it was abandoned.

The Alford & Sutton Railway was remarkable in that it succeeded in setting up in business at all. The Act was passed on 12th August 1880 and construction began straightaway by Messrs. B. Dick & Company. Mr. Dick was the owner of the tramway. The line started outside Alford station and ran along public roads until it reached the terminus at the Jolly Bacchus Inn. There were eleven passing places. The promotion of the Mablethorpe line brought about its end and closure took place in December 1889 after only six years of operation. Sadly, the outfit was offered to Alford Council for £500; they offered £300 but nothing further transpired thereafter. As its life was so short, it is convenient to relate its complete history here.

The offices and works of the company were opposite Alford railway station on the north side. A single line ran in front of the station and the first passing loop was in the roadway outside. The other loops were in strategic positions with a long one near Alford Church, two apiece at Markby and Bilsby and one each at Hannah and Thorpe road end. The railway was crossed on the level, and then followed a stub line to the engine shed on the south side and a final loop at the terminus.

Three 0-4-0 locomotives were used, and each different.

No.1 was vertical boilered, built by Black, Hawthorn & CO. of Gateshead in 1883. 7¼ in. x 11in. cylinders drove 2ft.3in. wheels.

No.2 had a horizontal Merryweather boiler, built in 1884 and with 7½ in. x 12in. cylinders driving 2ft.4in. wheels.

No.3 was a Dick, Kerr product of 1885. Built by the Britannia Engineering Co. of Kilmarnock having a loco. type boiler with 7in. x 12in. cylinders driving 2ft.4in. wheels.

The 'Lincolnshire Chronicle' for 4th April 1884 made the following reference to the opening of the line:

'The Alford and Sutton Tramway was publicly opened on Wednesday last. A committee of tradesman of Alford worked most energetically in decorating the town, and their work was tasteful and successful. Never has there been so much public spirit shown, and certainly no expense has been spared. Party coloured poles, bearing flags, banners and word allusions to the event of the day were everywhere displayed. The town was crowded with visitors and the tram cars were crowded on each of their successive journeys. The Alford Volunteer Bank and the Excelsior Brass Band enlivened the day's proceedings by their excellent playing, and accompanied the cars to Sutton. An excellent knife and fork tea was provided by Host Hibbitt in the Corn Exchange.'

Further gems of reporting appeared in the same newspaper for the following week:

'The day's programme indicated (2nd April 1884) that cars would leave Alford railway station for Markby Bridge at 10 and 11.30 a.m.; that the first cars for Sutton and back would leave Alford Market Bridge at 12.15 p.m., returning from Sutton at 1.20 p.m.; that the second cars would leave the Market Place at 2.30 p.m.; and that the third cars would leave at five o'clock, to convey returning passengers, leaving Sutton for Alford at six o'clock. The Sutton passengers were restricted to returning by the five o'clock cars. This trial of strength on the part of the tramway had been looked forward to in the district with considerable interest, for it was only in the previous few days its proprietors met the promoters of the Sutton and Willoughby Railway Bill in opposition, before a committee of the House of Commons, where it was contended that not only could the tramway undertake the ordinary traffic of the district, including heavy agricultural traffic, but that they would be able to deal with excursion passengers and the conveyance of heavy goods, including fish from the intended docks at Sutton! The opening day's performance did not, however, bear out this contention on the part of the owners of the tramway to a very brilliant degree. The first tram appointed to leave Alford for Markby at 10 a.m. left at 11.15, and managed to get off the line on the way, causing a considerable amount of delay; the first cars arrived at Sutton an hour and a half later than the published time for returning to Alford. The second cars followed within a quarter of an hour, and returned almost immediately. The passengers who came down to Sutton by the third cars took the precaution of remaining in their seats in order to avoid the risk of having to walk or hire traps to convey them home. This, according to the terms of the public notices, should have completed the day's programme, but there remained the awkward question, how the number of passengers still left at Sutton should be conveyed back to Alford? After hours of waiting, an open car and two open trucks used for carrying road materials arrived and were placed at the disposal of the wearied and impatient passengers. The spectacle of several ladies having to climb up into an open truck and there to settle themselves for a journey of six or seven miles on a chilly night, after ten o'clock, was not very suggestive of civilisation. Not only was the clause in the Tramway Act, which 'exempts the company on failing to convey passengers who may wish to travel by their line' fully taken advantage of, whereby a large number of people who wished to travel to Sutton were left behind, including several who had taken tickets, but it took the whole day with the two engines and including the use of the two trucks and all the available force of the tramway proprietors to convey 250 people a journey of about 6½ miles and back, the last tram not arriving at its destination until midnight.'

The line did however merit a little praise in the same edition:

'On Monday last a pony trap belonging to Mrs. Simons of Sutton was conveying a gentleman through the town of Alford when, on passing the shop of Mr. Lewis one of the trap wheels fell off, and the odd spectacle of a travelling one-wheeled trap was exhibited for a short distance. The pony was very shortly pulled up and the convenience of the Alford & Sutton Tramway was immediately and conclusively shewn, for the passenger by the disabled trap stepped into a passing tram and was conveyed to his destination, the Bacchus Hotel at Sutton, without loss or hindrance.'

In view of past machinations the MS & L, later the GCR, could not expect to find itself in splendid isolation with a monopoly in the crossing of the Trent. It is will be recalled that the L & Y and GER had designs on foreign parts earlier in the history of the railways of Lincolnshire, and the L & Y in particular would dearly have loved to link up its system with the south side of the Humber at Winteringham. It already enjoyed running powers into Hull via Goole on the north bank. For this purpose some 300 acres were brought from the Lord Carrington of the time and a jetty was planned there. The nearest the L & Y were to the Trent was over the Axholme Joint Railway which they shared with the NER, a rural affair made up of the Goole & Marshland and Isle of Axholme Light Railways, acquired by them in 1902. The line ran from near Goole to

Reedness Jc. in the middle of nowhere, and from there the main route ran south across the MS & L at Crowle to join the GN & GE Joint at Haxey. There were two branches, one to Hatfield and the other to Fockerby from Reedness Jc., quite near to the Trent bank. It was all sugar beet and potatoes, but the underlying plot was to cross the river and join up with the New Holland to Barton branch.

The Trent Valley Light Railway of 1900, known as the Blyton & Frodingham, was a strong contender with designs on the ironstone mines, but was written off after seven years.

The L & Y produced a second scheme out of the hat, this time to run a light railway from Ackworth, near Pontefract, to Fockerby, then under the Trent in tunnel and along to Barton. The GCR set out schemes of their own, the first being the North Lindsey Light Railway with the broad aim of connecting

Opening of Axholme Railway.   *Hull Libraries*

Scunthorpe with the Humber. The Act was incorporated in 1900 and one of the interested parties was the local landowner Sir Berkeley Sheffield who was a GCR Director, so it was certain that his company would be in favour and did in fact help to raise capital and operated the line from the outset in return for 60% of the revenue. The first section of six miles ran from a triangular junction east of Frodingham station to Dawes Lane, the principal station, Winterton & Thealby and West Halton, this section opening on 3rd September 1906. There were three trains each way on weekdays. On 13th July 1907 the 2½ mile West Halton to Winteringham section was opened. This was followed by a similar distance from Winteringham to Whitton on 1st December 1910. A single line ran from Normanby Park North signal box to Whitton, serving the wharves at Winteringham. The GCR had also put down plans for extensions from Winteringham to Barton and from Whitton to Burton Stather, though it is most likely that these were no more than devices to block L & Y encroachment. The GCR did, however, work L & Y coal traffic from their own jetty! The first train out to Winteringham was a sports club outing on 13th July 1907 carrying 254 passengers; probably the number was never exceeded again. By 1922 things had been reduced to one train each way until the service was withdrawn from 13th July 1925.

A ferry ran between Winteringham Haven and Hull, out Mondays and return on Wednesdays which hardly offered much scope. The Hull-Gainsborough steamer called at Whitton Pier three times weekly. In spite of healthy freight working the line remained single, nor was the extension to Barton, last mentioned in 1913, proceeded with.

As the chief contender against the GCR for traffic in North Lincolnshire, it is worth considering more detail the various ruses by which the L & Y sought to make its presence felt in the area. All manner of proposals were made and these stemmed firstly from a quarrel with Goole Town Council over the rates charged at the Docks, with a resultant wish to look elsewhere for a better port with a deeper draught (Grimsby was in their minds) and secondly from a desire to reach the potentially lucrative ironstone fields.

The first of the schemes was the Ackworth & Lindsey Light Railway of November 1904 which was to run from Ackworth station (NE & Midland Joint) crossing the H & BR near Kirk Smeaton, then via Sykehouse, Marshland Jc. where there would be a connection with the Axholme Joint Railway, Swinefleet, Adlingfleet, then a tunnel beneath the Trent and so on to Whitton where a spur would reach the North Lincs. line, Winteringham, South Ferriby and independently through Barton to cross the New Holland line at Goxhill with a spur and then to East Halton where the line was to divide into two, one spur running east to North Killingholme Haven, the other south east to join the Humber Commercial Railway of 1902 and Dock. The cost of the scheme was to be £585,523, of which £78,000 was for the tunnel. It was apparent that the line was to be worked by electricity on the overhead system, looking like a tramway. There was keen opposition to the scheme which was, perhaps unfortunately, defeated. The GCR objected to the likely infiltration by the H & BR, the Midland and the NER into the area, while the latter realised that it would weaken their own hold on the port of Hull.

A further scheme of the L & Y was an attempt to take over the NLLR by suitable inducements such as running powers over an extension from Fockerby, on the Axholme Joint Railway. However, the NLLR was too involved with the GCR to fall for such blandishments. The GCR viewed with suspicion the AJR which, ostensibly an agricultural line, was nevertheless seen as an attack upon them by the L & Y and NER. The NLLR had proposed an extension of their line to Fockerby via Alkborough from Whitton-the means of crossing the Trent not specified-upon which the L & Y proposed in turn to obtain access to their jetty at Winteringham. Mr. Aspinall, the General Manager, did not think that they would make much headway as the NER were bound to be involved as partners in the AJR. The NLLR, one of whose Directors was an L & Y man, sought to strengthen their position by playing off the L & Y and the GCR against each other, in one case by hinting that they would welcome a take-over by the former company. In September 1906 Mr. Simpson for the NLLR contacted Mr. Parmiter of the L & Y and said that they were prepared to grant running powers to any independent company who promoted a railway from Fockerby to Alkborough, and that they would consider the sale of the NLLR outright to the L & YR.

Strong stuff for the GCR to take, though the L & Y seemed to have been cautious. The GCR offered to take on the construction of the proposed line to Barton, for which assurances were sought, and asked for support in raising further capital, in particular with the construction of Winteringham Haven Pier. The land was already in directors' hands, about fourteen acres for which these shrewd gentlemen were asking £15,000. The GCR suggested half the sum as the true value, and offered to complete the works and necessary connections.

Still buoyant, the L & Y came up with another proposal, dated November 1906 for a railway of theirs from Fockerby to Alkborough. The feature here was a bridge over the Trent of eight arches, including an 80ft. swing span. The clearance when closed was to be 13ft. The Bill sought running powers over the NLLR and powers to construct wharves at Winteringham.

It is interesting that, among the backers of the NLLR, as well as Sebastian W. Meyer, the L & Y 'mole', was the Lord Carrington of the day.

In the following January in came the NER opposing the L & Y scheme, as it would be detrimental to their interests in Hull, where they had hitherto accommodated the L & Y. The L & Y did get an option to build at Winteringham, putting forward as chief reason for this necessity the problems caused to their shipping by silting of the upper channel to Goole.

The GCR responded to the action of the L & Y as follows, as shown in the Board Meeting minutes dated 6th February 1907 and the report of Dixon Davis:

'As soon as we heard rumours of the L & Y proposals we reopened the negotiations with the directors of the NLLR and the result has been that an amended agreement has recently been concluded under which the GCR are to work the whole of the Light Railway, including the extensions of 1905 and the railway and Pier proposals by this company's Bill. The last mentioned works sanctioned are to be constructed forthwith by the North Lindsey company. To enable them to do this the GCR are to subscribe £125,000 to their capital and this subscription will enable the GCR to control that company. This agreement further provides that the NLLR shall not lease or grant running powers over any part of their property without the consent of this company. This agreement we propose to confirm by the GCR Bill. The manorial rights in the Haven itself, together with some 14 acres of land adjacent there to have been recently sold by Lord Carrington to certain directors on the NLLR. As this land and the Haven are included within the limits of the land to be acquired, both by the NLLR and this company, and as the North Lindsey have deposited a light railway order which is now pending before the Commission, the ownership of this position becomes one of strategic importance.'

'The L & Y ask for compulsory running powers over the whole of the NLLR system and for powers to subscribe such moneys as they think fit to that undertaking, and to take up and hold any debenture stock of the company, while they further provided that the NER may also join it in exercising the powers of construction and running referred to.'

'We are of course taking every means directly and indirectly to defeat the threatened invasion of our territory and interests. We shall not be alone in our opposition, for the injury which the proposed must cause to the navigation of the Trent has already aroused widespread opposition from all parties concerned in the extensive traffic now carried on the river.'

'It is a dangerous innovation for a line which was acquired as an agricultural railway to be converted into a predatory attack upon another company's district.'

It is recorded that Goole UDC and the L & Y and NER opposed the GCR Bill. The hue and cry raised over the proposed Trent Bridge was much greater, with eleven authorities opposing it. As in many cases of the kind, a compromise was reached, and a the GCR Board Meeting of 12th April 1907 the following was reported:

'Negotiations have taken place between the General Manager, Mr. Fay, and the L & Y. In the event of the final agreement being arrived at with the L & Y, the opposition to our Bill regarding the NLLR will become relatively unimportant.

1. The GCR will not enroach upon on interfere with L & Y property at Winteringham.

2. The GCR agree to the L & Y connecting their property by sidings to the NLLR.

3. The L & Y to agree to work all traffic as they would do their own(!).

4. The L & Y not to construct or assist in any way in the promotion of sidings or lines in competition with the NLLR, the intention being that in exchange for the facilities given by the GCR to the L & Y, the GCR or NLLR shall not be deprived of the traffic they were designed to carry.

5. The GCR to agree to all traffic arising upon or destined for the NLLR and the railways running from Winteringham towards Whitton and Barton from stations on the L & Y or beyond being exchanged at Doncaster and receipts divided by either the Doncaster or Askern route or accounted for as exchanged. This agreement to be in perpetuity.

6. The GCR not to object to any application made by the L & Y for authority to construct a Pier at Winteringham under the Steam Vessels Act 1904.'

The astute L & Y had of course secured a stronger position for themselves by threatening to erect the dreaded and unlikely bridge. The Aire & Calder Canal Company who would have been affected by obstruction to their traffic on the Trent, reduced L & Y levies for coal cartage by £4,000 per annum; Ouse tolls were reduced, Goole Dock dues for continental sailings were reduced and 25% was lifted from water charges levied on the use of hydraulic machinery. In August 1907 the Bill promoting the Pier at Winteringham and its ancilliaries received Assent.

The story is not yet over. In 1909 the Trent, Railway, Road & Bridge Company reared its head, possibly sponsored by the L & Y but not overtly so. The plan was for a rail-cum-road bridge, the one from Fockerby to Alkborough, the other from Garthorpe. The crossing was to be at Island House Sands on five arches of forty feet, then one of 164ft. and the two final arches of 90ft. swing spans. This must have been a scheme which was most unsure of itself, as in the following year further Deposited Plans show another bridge one quarter of a mile south of the above with nine arches of 140ft. and the two smaller swing spans. The schemes were real enough to attract capital of £132,000 and a five year run to completion. However, opposition came from every quarter except the L & Y and the schemes were dropped.

First Passenger Train, Winterton/Scunthorpe. 1906   *Hull Libraries*

    One very effective and heavily used bridge existed over the Trent, the swing span over which Mr. Joshua Slowen of Barnetby had driven the first train in 1853. The bridge was carrying a great volume of traffic up to the Great War, with all the main line trains from Liverpool, Manchester and Sheffield, and a great tonnage of coal and iron ore in each direction between Scunthorpe and Immingham and the Midlands.

Keadby Bridge and Barge, early 1920's.   *Hull Libraries*

In 1910 a scheme was prepared to build a new bridge some 58 chains north of the old one, including a diverted railway. The first Bill was withdrawn, due to the same vigorous local landowners who had been active in blocking the other plans. Eventually, however, authority was gained to construct the new bridge on a site adjacent to the old one, the railway company undertaking to give a clear river passage of 150ft., more generous than the earlier one of 120 ft. which had needed a central pier and dolphin. A Royal Commission on canals and waterways had had an eye on the position at the lower end of the Trent, and stressed the importance of the river to Nottingham. One more here which must have impressed was the offer by the railway to provide a roadway alongside the lines.

Work began on the deviation railway of two miles running parallel to the original route some 200ft. on the north side. The work went ahead smoothly on both banks which were linked by pilot steam tug. The river flowed at 5-7 knots, with a periodic bore or 'eagre' which surged at 15 mph. The normal rise and fall of the water was 14ft. and 18ft. was afforded under the fixed spans at high tide. There were five of these, covering a total length of 548ft. and resting on caissons filled with concrete driven to 50ft. below low water. The total weight of steel used was 2,760 tons.

The great feature of the bridge was its lift span, operated on the Scherzer principle by which motors set on the leaf itself engaged spur gears on to toothed racks 40ft. long to give a precise opening angle of 81° 51.

Keadby Bridge from signal cabin, looking towards Althorpe.   *C. T. Goode*

A 50 hp. petrol engine was installed on the Up side near the bridge working two 115 hp. 220 volt DC motors which took two minutes to complete the movement. Hand winches were also provided, but how long these took is not recorded! On Sunday, 31st October 1915, ten months after commencement, ten men did winch down the lifting span which had been built upright to leave the river free of clutter. At first the counterweight, which ended up a mere three inches above the rail tops when 'up' was found to be too heavy, due to water present the concrete mix. Then, on 7th November 1915 the span of 987 tons was lowered, this time by four men who found that it stopped half an inch short of the horizontal with a ⅝th twist to the north, hardly noticeable but enough to cause consternation. All was put to rights in due course and by 22nd December 1916 the auxiliary batteries were working which could give thirty movements of the span before charging. Normal bridge lifts were five movements daily, so that one charge weekly would be ample. Weather conditions caused great variants in current use; in gales up to 1,700 amps. would be needed in three minutes against an average of 855 amps. in normal use, while it is said that, with the wind in the right quarter, the span would almost lift without power up to 45°!

Train of timber from Immingham Dock, headed by N5. No 69305. (Eastern Region)
C. T. Goode

Easy it is to run riot over detail with structures of this kind, but several items are worth noting. Masts of 110ft. were erected on each side of the river to carry signalling equipment across when the span was raised. The broken rail joints came down into steel shoes for correct alignment, the expansion gap being 1 3/16 in. In position the bridge was secured by two 8in. x 2in. electrically worked bolts, while in the centre was a big pneumatic buffer to cushion the descent of the span if things got out of hand. The counterweight was 1,800 tons of concrete on a box of steel plates across the back of the span. The engineer called it his 'monolithic mass.' The signalling was housed

New Holland Train at Immingham Dock. D11 62662 "Princess Mary".

C. T. Goode

in a cabin on the north side with 28 levers controlling road, rail and water. As well as the usual arms was a hand worked ball signal. The lifting leaf was the heaviest in Europe when built; the roadway on it was of dowelled jarrah paving blocks on pitch pine planking ten inches thick, while the footpath was of creosoted pitch pine for lightness. An 8ft. close boarded fence kept rail and road apart. The bridge was opened on 21st May 1916 with Driver Slowen on board the 10.35 a.m. from Althorpe with 250 guests. The last train over the old bridge left Scunthorpe at 9.55 a.m.

At about this time Logan & Hemingway filled in the arches of the Scotter Road viaduct.

The new Immingham Dock was to be served by three new railways, and in this corner of Lincolnshire their growth was not to be complicated by schemes which did not materialise. First on the scene was the Grimsby District Light Railway which was originally thought out during 1902 but which did not harden into a firm Act until 15th January 1906. With electric traction in mind the line was to lead off the Grimsby tramway system by a triangular junction, across Corporation Bridge and then run for 5¾ miles to the edge of the Dock estate. A connection was to be effected with the main line at Marsh Jc. near Great Coates station, again by a triangular junction, the branch meeting the light railway end-on but then veering off eastwards into the timber yards. The GDLR was opened in May 1906 and was used by trains conveying materials, special workings of passenger trains and by dock employees. Soon it was realised that the public could well benefit from the line, so that from 3rd January 1910 the GCR put on a steam railcar service between two wooden termini, namely Pyewipe Road dep; 8.45 a.m., 12 noon, 3.0 p.m. and 5.45 p.m., and Immingham Halt dep: 9.10 a.m., 12.30 p.m., 3.30 p.m. and 6.10 p.m. taking 20 minutes. Fares were 6d return, workmen 4d. Of course, the normal contractor's trains continued to run as well. On the opening of Immingham loco. depot this line was used to despatch and receive light engines to and from Grimsby.

Not far from Immingham the Habrough-New Holland line ran to the west, and two other lines serving the docks were taken from it. The Humber Commercial Railway struck out eastwards north of Ulceby station and the northern tip of the triangular layout bringing traffic from east and west. So important was the line that it was pressed into service on 3rd January 1910 to serve the Western Jetty with coal. At Humber Road Jc. a line branched south and linked up with the third line mentioned below. This served the other side of the dock area and ended in a triangular junction with the abovementioned GDLR and a passenger terminal.

In order to bring the New Holland traffic to Immingham, the Barton and Immingham Light Railway was opened in two stages, the first from Immingham West Jc. to Killingholme on 1st December 1910 and to the junction at Goxhill on 1st May 1911. By now the GCR had financially overplayed its hand somewhat, and no part of the final stage from Goxhill to Barton was commenced, not surprising in view of the presence of the perfectly functional Barton branch. The line, unlike the Ulceby branch, was single. Passenger services on the Barton and Immingham began on 2nd May 1911 between New Holland and Immingham West Jetty, and intermediate stations were built at East Halton and Killingholme. Approximately seven trains each way ran on weekdays.

The last of the lines to serve the docks at Immingham was probably the most famous, the Grimsby & Immingham Tramway, known also as the Grimsby & District Electric Railway. For convenience of reference all the details of the line are included at this point. The line was sanctioned under the Grimsby Light Railway Order of 1906 and contracts were awarded to Messrs. Price, Wills & Reeves in 1909 whereby, for £11,360 they would construct a tramway on the landward side of the Grimsby District from Pyewipe to Immingham. For a further £16,474 they would erect all overheads, bond the rails and supply three substations through which the 6,600 volts AC supply taken from the docks would be converted to 500 volts DC. The line ran from Corporation Bridge in Grimsby to Immingham, was 5⅜ miles long and not connected to the steam line. The line was inspected for fitness on 22nd November 1911, but not opened until 15th May 1912, after the Dock had been in use for a time. The speed limits in forces were 12mph. in streets and 25mph. in the open. The run took twenty minutes, the same as the steam rail motor which was withdrawn on the opening of the tramway. The single fare was 5d. and on the first day of running things were so busy that the ticket stock ran out. The 30ft. rails were flat bottomed on ash sleepers at first but later replaced by bull-head which gave a rougher ride. At the Grimsby end there was originally a booking office and waiting room, while at the Immingham end the terminus was called 'Town', later 'Halt', and was ¾ mile from the village. There were originally fourteen passing places, though the line began as double track from Corporation Bridge to Cleveland Bridge, the cars running in standard 45ft. grooved rails in granite setts. There were six

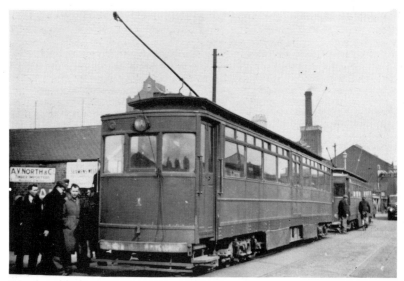

Grimsby and Immingham car No. 1 at Cleveland Bridge, Grimsby.　　　C. T. Goode

passing loops in the Grimsby section, with important ones at Yarborough Street, Beeson Street, Cleveland Street and possibly at Stortford Street.

The eight 'country' passing places were suitably fenced off and fitted with cattle guards where necessary, entered through spring loaded points indicated by electric lamps. The overhead wire was supported by span wires across the road up to the Recreation Ground, then by bracket arms. Maintenance was carried at Pyewipe Depot where two cars could be housed in the main building and a further one in the paint shop. Outside were three sidings, one with an inspection pit.

The original service was generous, with the first car leaving Grimsby at 5.10 a.m., then three others at 5 minute intervals and an hourly service to 7.15 p.m. The first return car left Immingham at 5.45 a.m., then hourly to 7.45 p.m. with extras over teatime. Some records give a half-hourly service, with an hourly headway during the night hours over a twenty-four hour period; no doubt the cars would run as dictated by the requirements of the work in hand at the docks.

Two extensions were laid down, the first on 17th November 1913 running to the eastern edge of the dock estate, then reversing to run in the roadway to the dock estate boundary and then over reserved track to the eastern jetty. This was a double track line with concrete masts and had a twenty minute service during at least one period of its life.

The second extension was a white elephant which ran from the same point as that above. Opened on 20th July 1915 it was demanded by Grimsby Council but not approved of by the GCR and consisted of a single line running to a passing loop near the engine sheds. The overhead was held by span wires and it is recorded that the line was in fact used for one week only and was not developed, in spite of petitions from the villagers to have it extended.

The line developed its own sort of lore, and the cars themselves developed a sagging appearance at each end the older they became, divided into smoking and non-smoking compartments and upon them could be found notices 'earnestly requesting passengers to refrain from spitting.' At Immingham Dock there were refreshment and dining rooms with sections for 1st, 2nd and 3rd Class passengers. The Author has never found any instance of a 3rd Class passenger imbibing tea in a 1st Class Buffet, and what in fact would the punishment for such an offence be? On Immingham Dock, again, the timetable was printed in seven different languages, namely English, Dutch, German, Swedish, Norwegian, Italian and Spanish.

Referring to the cars themselves, these were standard gauge and were originally sixteen in number, single deck double bogied vehicles, Nos. 1-12 built by the Brush Electrical Engineering Co., and Nos. 13-16 by the GCR. The standard vehicles had two 50hp motors and seated 60 passengers. Nos. 1-4 and 9-16 were identical in appearance with a weight of 15 tons, while 5-8 were similar but in fact smaller with 35hp motors and seating 40 passengers. To take the history of the cars through to closure, Nos. 6-8 were scrapped in 1931, No.5 becoming a Works car. By 1948 13 cars had reached British Railways and these were augmented by ex Newcastle cars Nos. 29,77 and 42 which took Nos.6-8. They were not successful and were stored at Pyewipe. In 1951 19 Gateshead cars were bought and took Nos. 17-34. One was damaged and used as a shed. In 1954 No. 34 took the place of No. 5 as Works car, and the first vehicles to be withdrawn were Nos. 2, 9, 10 and 13. No. 10 also became a sort of shed. In 1955 all the Gateshead cars were in BR green, while two Newcastle cars and the older standard cars remained in rather drab LNER brown.

To expedite repairs a shed had been built at No 2 Passing Place where servicing could be done on site and bogies exchanged. Vehicles were often left out in the open at both ends when not in use.

Grimsby Corporation exercised its right under the original 1906 Act to purchase the section of line between Corporation and Cleveland Bridges from the railway company, so that from 30th June 1956 motor buses were put on. From September 1959 services were reduced to three hours on weekdays mornings and two hours Mon-Fri and midday Sat. Closure was scheduled for September 1961, provided that a new road link was built between Grimsby and Immingham.

The logical starting point from which to enter North Lincs. on the old GCR system is Retford, though that town is of course in Nottinghamshire and in fact the former county is not reached until the Trent is crossed near Gainsborough. Originally the MS & L had its own station at Retford, east of the flat crossing with the GNR, a fine building built, like that at Worksop, by Thomas Hutchins & Co. of Anston. Retford was a long, single storey building with two storeyed towers at each end and with a centre three arched porte cochere. This was flanked by eight deep windows, four on each side. The building here cost £10,710, which was in the event an expensive investment as the station was dispensed with as early as 1859 when trains began to use the GN station. Worksop cost £7,800 and still survives as a fine monument to the architect and builder.

For ease of connection all trains used the new GN station. The spur round to the east from the GN was left in, and a new loop was put in from Whisker Hill (a corruption of 'West Carr') to bring the Sheffield trains in at the north end where for many years they were to harass East Coast expresses on occasion. The original run across the GN on the flat was left in for goods trains and passenger services not stopping at Retford. Latterly the ex GNR Class K2s were often seen and heard clattering across the crossing on excursions.

Running north east there were three signal cabins in the vicinity of Retford, at Thrumpton Crossing, Gringley and Welham Road. From the latter there was a long rise at 1 in 120 up a big embankment on which trains needed a banking engine from time to time. As the summit was neared the line turned eastwards to run into Clarborough tunnel at 3 miles 130yd from Retford South. Here the Gainsborough line ran north east, leaving the short link to Sykes Jc. on the GN & GE Joint line to run straight ahead. Thus a quite unpretentious junction in fact selected either Lincoln of Cleethorpes as the destination of all traffic from the west. Clarborough village lay well back to the west on the north side of the line and was linked to the neighbouring village of Hayton along a road leading to the Chesterfield canal.

The link to Sykes Jc. was almost 8¼ miles long and fell at the ruling gradient of 1 in 120 for 2½ miles, running in a south easterly direction, first passing between the villages of North and South Leverton, whose station was situated on the gradient-usually a level stretch is managed in station limits. The premises were within a short distance of the villages served. Almost two miles further on the line levelled out as it reached the valley of the Trent and approached Cottam, a small village just north of the line and otherwise remote from civilisation. In 1885 there was only one siding on the north side of the line east of the level crossing, the station lying to the west of this.

At just over a mile from Cottam the line crossed the Trent on a low bridge approached from each side on low runs of 1 in 100. This had been constructed to the designs of John Fowler, later to design the Forth Bridge, and had in fact been regarded dubiously by the Inspecting Officer before opening. However, Fowler got his way and the two span wrought iron structure survived. Thereafter the line entered Torksey, the third and last station on the line. The total cost of erecting them was a mere £320, and they dated from 1853. The station here was isolated, with Abbey ruins nearby for company. North of the line was a long goods siding west of the platforms, served by a connection at each end. A goods shed was provided. The village of Torksey is a small one on the river bank and enjoyed historical importance as the point where the Fossdyke joined the Trent, attracting first the Danes who travelled upriver, then priories, a castle and lastly the golf course on the north side of the line where battles of a different kind are fought. The final run of 2m.793yd. to Sykes Jc. was south east over a gently rising gradient.

Trains passing through Cottam station in 1874 were as follows:-

To Lincoln. 1.23a.m. Express Goods, 9.06a.m., 9.18a.m. Goods, 10.26a.m.(FO), 10.53a.m., 12.38p.m., 2.48p.m.(SO) stops on request, 5.40p.m., 7.48p.m., 9.00p.m. Express cattle, 11.58p.m. Goods. Sundays:- 11.08a.m., 7.28p.m. To Retford:- 3.45a.m. and 4.05a.m. Goods, 7.52a.m.,11.05a.m., 12.05p.m. Pick-up, 3.09p.m. XP non-stop, 3.50p.m. Pick-up, 4.24p.m., 6.26p.m. Sundays:- 10.01a.m., 5.56p.m.

The 1949 timetable shows much more traffic using the line than above, with 6-7 stopping trains in each direction between Lincoln and either Retford or Sheffield, and with several interesting freight trains such as the 9.26p.m. Northwich-Whitemoor, the 1.15a.m. Dewsnap-Lincoln, 11.45p.m. Liverpool (Brunswick)-Whitemoor and the 8.00p.m. Cowbit-Sheffield Vic. XP Parcels. This was an oddity in that the original train left Whitemoor for York double headed, and the Sheffield portion and engine were split at Cowbit for some reason, instead of Boston. There were also the summer Saturday excursions and the Harwich-Liverpool expresses in each direction. In 1981 3-4 oil trains passed along the line to and from Immingham.

To return to the Gainsborough route from Clarborough Jc. This struck off north east and basically fell to the bank of the Trent with a sharp initial drop at 1 in 120 for almost two miles. Sturton station was reached at 2 miles 225yd. and was the only intermediate stopping place between here and Gainsborough. Sturton-le-Steeple village was quite sizeable, lying east of the station, while not too far away on the opposite side was the even larger settlement of North and South Wheatley. The later power station of West Burton was sited beyond here to the west by the river and connected by double junctions for each direction. Opposite was the village of Bole which never had a station, probably due to its proximity to the A620, though its name is mentioned from time to time in the chronicle of railway projects.

The MS & L crossed the Trent first and soon had for company the other jointly owned route between Lincoln and Doncaster, giving a junction at each side of the river crossing. The Trent crossing here was another Fowler effort with a run-up viaduct from the west side, made of wood leading on to two hollow girder spans of 154ft., the total length, including run-up spans and abutments totalling 460ft. Six engines and various vehicles were all marshalled together to test the structure, which was found to be extremely adequate. With two junctions to contend with, one on each bank, it would seem that two signal boxes would be called for, as in indeed was originally the case. Later on there was a tall wooden cabin working both sets of points at the north side on the east bank; with motor points and a fixed span there was no great problem. Ultimately the layout was modernised and a brick cabin provided. The Trent is sinuous here and turns sharply to pursue the line due north into Gainsborough Central station.

The town numbered around 18,000 at the turn of the century and had grown into an industrial centre for the manufacture of machinery and farm implements. It had been important since Anglo-Saxon times when King Alfred married there. Young Canute the Dane commenced his operations from there in 1014. Keen Civil War fighting took place here in the 17th century and one notable battle was between the Royalist Charles Cavendish and Cromwell himself.

The rail battles here were not so fierce, though the rival companies kept themselves apart at each end of the town. The Central station, a noble affair costing £18,000 lay to the east on embankment where the MS & L line curved northwards, the layout of the sidings being constrained by the elevation. These were chiefly on the town side, the first group at West signal box with an extension to engineering works. Then came the platforms, followed by East cabin; both boxes were on the same side of the running lines. East supervised the goods yard, warehouses with four cranes and a coal yard on the east side. In the coal yard was a small blacksmith's forge and a stable for three horses. The station building was impressive, having a long frontage consisting of a central square portico with four pillars flanked by a single storey building on each side terminated at each end by square two storey blocks to match the centre. These were rendered particularly distinguished by having the roof beams projecting with decorated ends below the eaves, and with stone quoins down the corners to offset the brickwork. Unfortunately the effect was ruined later when the sidings were linked from either side in front of the approach, necessitating a subway for pedestrians and causing the addition of a lean-to made of wood for weather protection. Sadly almost everthing has gone today, except for a couple of bus shelters on the platforms, the old footbridge and old West cabin which survives at the time of writing to preside over the stub of line which was the loading dock and a few adjacent sidings serving the Britannia Works. Even the adjacent engineering premises area abandoned and derelict, adding to the sad picture. The station sees seven trains daily on weekdays.

The line swung round Gainsborough to the north, passing two of its schools and then bore north east after crossing the Scunthorpe road to pass Thonock Sidings box. A visit to the site today would give away nothing of the great activity here at one time, caused by the opening in February 1918 of a Filling Factory north of the line by the Ministry of Munitions. In 1920 the factory employed 209 people breaking down bombs and mines to extract ammonium nitrate. Sidings were laid down, and a platform was provided for the staff. No record exists of when the premises closed, but the railway was left with one long refuge road for each direction at Thonock.

After about five miles from Gainsborough, the line entered Blyton station, and with the capriciousness found in such cases, the station was placed, not by the main road and village to the north of it, but some way east near the hamlet of Pilham. Here were the usual offices, with a goods depot, signal box and station buildings on the north side and a lay-by siding with cattle pens on the south. The RAF had a base at Blyton during the 1939-45 War.

Northorpe station came next (3m) and served the village lying down the road to the west, itself being somewhat isolated. Northorpe Hall was also, to be found, an interesting place in that the owner built himself a modern one next to the original Elizabethan version. Originally Northorpe station had only a small goods yard on the north side; however, this was later embellished by lay-by sidings for each direction. The aptly named river Eau flowed beneath the railway at this point, en route to the Trent.

Some 2½ miles beyond Northorpe came Kirton Lindsey station, serving the small and busy town of little streets situated a mile away from the line on the slope of the hills. In the 18th century the area was part of the Duchy of Cornwall. As befitted a more important place the site had more to offer, with a huge warehouse and several sidings all on the south side with coal drops and overlooked by the sonorous Binns, Tickler & Richardson Flour Mill. On the northbound platform trains could take refreshment before tackling the 1 in 132 up through Kirton tunnel of 1,334yd. which brought them up past Parry's Lime Works ruled by a tall signal cabin. To assist heavily loaded trains Retford provided a banking engine from 9.00a.m. Mon to 10.00p.m. Sat., stationed at Kirton Lindsey, the engine also shunting at the quarries when not required.

The straight course of Roman Ermine Street was crossed by means of a simple crossing plus keeper and manually operated gates; then came Scawby & Hibaldstow station (2m), north and south of the line respectively. Scawby is virtually an exclusive suburb of Scunthorpe and Brigg. Hibaldstow, whose church is dedicated to St. Hibald with a new tower, lay much nearer the railway. The station buildings were on the north side, the goods yard on the same side at the west end with the signal box opposite.

After crossing the A15 on the level, the line reached Brigg station (1½m) originally Glanford Brigg, once a fishing village on the Ancholme, then becoming a busy town with markets and food and agricultural factories. The station was originally largish with an overall roof, a porticoed front and with the stationmaster's quarters at the Grimsby end of the premises which faced towards the town. The site was well placed for its customers. There were ample coal sidings and facilities for general goods and cattle, though no refuge siding was provided.

After running north east for almost two miles, the line arrived at the vast intersection of Wrawby Jc. as the centre one of the three convergences.

Wrawby Jc.   *C. T. Goode*

The old GN 'road from Peterborough to Grimsby was very distinctive in character, retaining its period flavour to the last with the old somersault signals and keeping the Stirling Singles in employment after they had been withdrawn from main line services. From Werrington Jc. up to a point south of Burgh-le-Marsh station the line was straight and level, the longest flat section being between mileposts 97½ and107½ where the line entered Boston. North of that town the line pursued its course with 'bumps' over water

47

The great mass of leverage inside Wrawby Jc.   *C. T. Goode*

courses, notably the Maud Foster Drain at 109 miles which lent its name to the little cabin on the west side which controlled the gates on the Coningsby road. There were isolated stations further north, at Sibsey a the end of the village astride the Horncastle road, Old Leake (113m) which had only an inn for company on an indifferent road crossing-anything called Leake was

Maud Foster signal box, Boston.   *C. T. Goode*

vaguely off to the east of the line-and East Ville, a small settlement hard by the station and out in the fen, 3¼ miles from Old Leake (117m). The place deserves special mention because of the immense amount of sugar beet that would be moved here, up to 60 wagons each day in block loads, all by hand forking into wagons. There were two long sidings on the up side, while on the down side or village side was the small goods yard, warehouse and long headshunt. The level crossing and signal box were at the north end of the parallel platforms, while the main building was on the down platform.

Between here and Little Steeping was Bellwater Jc., the cabin set on the west side controlling the connection with the much later shortcut via Coningsby. Little Steeping (120m) proved to be no grander than the others. The station building was left of the line, the signal cabin on the right, serving a straggling hamlet on the minor road running north to, surprisingly enough, Great Steeping. The name comes from the Steeping river which flows into the Wash at Gibraltar Point.

Firsby looking South.   *H. C. Casserley*

Firsby (122m) was a grand place where the Skegness line went off to the east, giving a glorious excuse for a fine triangular layout with embellishments due to the taking off of the Spilsby branch westwards. All this took place south of the station proper, and holiday makers could pass round the south curve without passing beneath Firsby's overall roof, looking somewhat like a bit of Doncaster station planted out in the fens. Here was essentially a changing point, one of those delightful layouts built for railwaymen as Trent, Afon Wen and Hellifield were. Firsby is a mere hamlet to the south with no traffic potential. The station was substantial, of three platforms with the two bay overall awnings covering the running lines and the main buildings on the west side. To the east out in the open was a bay for Skegness and Spilsby trains. The layout here was controlled by cabins at North and South ends and at the Station cabin which worked the crossing gates at the Boston end of the platforms. The North cabin controlled the up refuge siding and was opened when required.

49

Departures from Firsby for the Skegness line, 1914:

7.10a.m., 8.47, 10.22 from Lincoln (reverses), 10.42 MO from Nottingham (reverses), 11.15, 12.52p.m., 1.45 from Grantham (reverses), 4.25, 5.28 from Lincoln (reverses), 6.45, 7.22 from Nottingham (reverses), 7.30, 9.25 SO. No Sunday trains.

Similar Departures for 1949:

7.13a.m., 8.44, 10.41 from Lincoln (reverse), 1.10p.m., 2.42 from Lincoln (reverses), 5.05, 6.30, 7.25 from Lincoln (reverses), 9.05. Sun. 10.51a.m., 4.05p.m., 6.56, 9.26.

In 1897 there were six trains each way daily, beginning with the 6.16a.m. Wainfleet-Skegness and ending with the 7.35p.m. Skegness-Wainfleet. Skegness station was revamped in 1936 and had three island and one side platform, seven faces in all with awnings to Nos. 3 & 4 only. Like other resorts Skegness grew enormously because of the railway which served it faithfully. Diesel units took over the branch from 1957 and after closure of the East Lincs. line including Firsby a dmu service was concentrated on the Nottingham-Grantham-Skegness route via Boston, taking the old south curve at Firsby which had an odd effect on the uninitiated due to the sudden change of direction for no apparent reason. The double tracked Boston-Skegness section was opened for only ten hours daily from 1977 and interavailability of bus and train tickets was introduced, though Saturday traffic demanded more trains. From 1981 part of the route became single track.

North of Firsby the line began to climb slightly to Burgh-le-Marsh (124½m), a site with parallel platforms and with all the main offices, warehouse, small crane, large cattle dock and signal box on the east side. From the level crossing at the north end the road ran east to Burgh at 2 miles distant, and Skegness, and west to Horncastle. There was a long down refuge siding at Burgh-le-Marsh, with a capacity for eighty wagons.

A long run, slightly undulating, of 3 miles 935yd followed to Willoughby where the line turned north west and where also the southern end of the Mablethorpe Loop came in from the north east. This was effected by means of the Junction signal box at the north end which was in section only while movements to or from the branch took place. The little village lay just east of the line by the level crossing, and is locally famed as the home of the Elizabethan voyager John Smith, founder of Virginia who was saved from death by Pocahontas, daughter of the hostile Indian chief. More mundanely, the station lay north of the crossing and was easily one of the best kept in Lincolnshire, a veritable garden of blooms in season. In 1924 the station won first prize in the Best Kept Stations Awards and gained fifteen others in successive years. Trains off the Loop were attended to in a bay on the Up side with a run-round line conveniently placed.

Diverting off the main line to the branch for convenience; this was divided into two working sections, namely Willoughby Jc.-Mablethorpe worked as a single line with the electric tablet, and from Mablethorpe-Louth by staff and ticket. First stop out of Willoughby was Mumby Road (3m), equidistant from Bilsby on one side and Mumby on the other. Here was a passing loop for summer use, a goods shed, crane and two sidings. A little over four miles further on came Sutton-on-Sea station with two platforms flanking a passing loop, sidings, a cattle dock and goods shed. Originally known as Sutton-le-Marsh, the quiet and restful little resort gained some unsought fame in 1953 when its sands were lost in the great break-through by the sea, causing

wholesale replacement by concrete defences. Mablethorpe, separated from Sutton by Trusthorpe, was 2¾ miles further north on the branch, and here was the biggest station on the branch with two bays facing Louth, relics of the days when the station was a terminus.
Here was a turntable, cattle dock, carriage siding, a brick warehouse and a small yard.

From Mablethorpe the line set off north west on its 13 mile run to Louth, passing the smallest station, Theddlethorpe with its single platform, one siding and ground frame. The two villages with the delightful names of Theddlethorpe All Saints and Theddlethorpe St. Helens lay on each side of the line on a minor road which crossed south of the station, and to protect buildings from the often severe winds which blow in these parts lines of trees can be noted, planted to screen them. At 5 miles the line turned rather smartly inland after crossing a road, to enter Saltfleetby station with its single platform and two sidings. The signal box here appears to have been opened only for the pickup goods to shunt. Saltfleet nearby was once a Royal Port with honourable mention in the Domesday Book, exporting grain and importing coal. Then the sea receded until the present situation where the low water mark is some two miles out and the village is in fact well inland. Round the station were three Saltfleetbys:- St. Clements, All Saints and St. Peter.

The line rose from Saltfleetby to Grimoldby (3m 932yd) where the little village was evident on both sides of the road crossing to the east of the single platform and siding. South of the line was the RAF base of Manby which would have generated much wartime traffic, though in all probability transport would have taken servicemen into Louth by road. After a further three miles the single line reached Mablethorpe Jc. on the direct line, the cabin open during branch operations only and within sight of Louth station. Excursion traffic normally all worked to and from Mablethorpe via the Willoughby end, leaving the northern section in relative obscurity.

Working over the Loop could involve either trips from north to centre, centre to south or right round, as witness the following table for 1949:

```
           a.m.
Louth   7.157.448.53   — 9.50        1000 — — — — 3.15 —       — 6.20
M'thorpe — — 9.18 9.25 1022          113512051.351.453.103.474.35 6.20 6.58
                                                                      p.m.
Sutton  7.45 — 9.29 9.33 1028        122212131.432.153.183.554.43 6.28 7.05
Will'by — 8.369.40 9.47 1042         1.00 12271.572.203.224.104.57 6.42 7.17
           to    to                  SO SO    to         to   to   to
         KingsX F'rsby               Nott'ham Man      Nott'm Nott'm F'rsby
                                              Cen
                                              SO       SX   SO
```

```
           a.m.                       p.m.
Will'by — 8.531018 11041133 11341213 1258 1.45 — 4.24   5.005.20 7.20 8.10
Sutton 8.089.071035 11201150 11511233 1.15 3.00 2.304.41 5.165.36 7.33 8.24
M'thrpe8.169.121040 11291155 11561238 1.20 3.08 2.374.46 5.255.41 7.38 8.29
Louth 8.45 —   — 1158 — — — — 5.10 3.02 —       5.54 — 8.06 9.01
       from from from from from from pick      from              from
       Nottm F'sbyNottm Leic NottmManc up      Nottm             F'sby
       SO          SX   SO  SO  SO good        SO
```

Motive power would be the smaller GNR tender locomotives, of which nine Class E1s were kept at Lincoln, then the C12 4-4-2 tanks. A point here is that the Mablethorpe turntable would take no bigger than a J6 or J11 0-6-0 tender engine, so that larger breeds were sent off in groups to turn on the Firsby triangle.

To return to the main line at Willoughby:- Running north for 2½ miles, Alford Town station was met with (130½m) serving the pleasant little market town on the east side of the line, once famed for its Bull Fair. Mention has been made of the tramway to Sutton-on-Sea which ran, during the short period of its existence, to the station yard. In that yard was a loading dock, five ton crane and warehouse, the latter only provided in later years. The pointwork was quite elaborate here, and shunting work could be done on both sides of the running lines. On the down side was a siding running behind the platform and a refuge siding for 44 wagons. The platforms were opposite each other, and both the station buildings and signal box were on the east side, the cabin set beyond the level crossing, causing some heavy lever movements as all the points would be at some distance.

The next three stations may be taken together before Louth is reached, as they were not very vigorous throughout their lives. Aby, one of the shortest station names to be found anywhere, (134m) on a skew level crossing serving the hamlets of Aby and Claythorpe on each side, Authorpe (135m) which served its small hamlet to the east and whose cabin was opened as required, and Legbourne Road (138½m), one of those little puzzles encountered occasionally which makes research interesting, for Legbourne was adjacent to the line on the east side and the rails passed over two level crossings, the southernmost of which was in the village and so handy for Little Cawthorpe on the other side. Perverseness prevailed, however, and the station was sited south of the other level crossing away from the village but probably bearing in mind the more important road. Two miles further on the line arrived at Mablethorpe Jc. to enter Louth station (141m).

Reference has been made to the importance of Louth as a centre for cattle and the impressive special trains ran certainly up to the 1939-45 war. The building itself was most imposing in the Elizabethan style, of brick with stone facings and quoins, stone mullions and transomed windows. The main features for the layman were the arched and pillared porte cochere, the gables with fancy rounded tops and a forest of finials, balls and Tudor chimneys. As often the case later embellishments at each end spoiled things. The station buildings faced the town on the west side of the line. There were two main platforms, the up side being an island to house the Mablethorpe and Bardney branch trains. On that side was a small locomotive depot (40C) with turntable and premises for servicing. Louth South cabin stood buried up to the waist in the up platform and dealt with movements at that end. The station had an overall roof like that at Firsby, that is, two bays with centre supporting pillars between the running lines. A subway linked the platforms, though this was quite likely a replacement for an earlier footbridge. At the time of writing the building still survives, albeit in a poor state as the only one of those from Boston. The atmosphere, even in ruin, is rich in former activity, indefinable yet dominating. Louth North box controlled Keddington Road level crossing from the east side, plus connections to the up yard, two factories and the rather large down goods yard with warehouse and ten ton crane.

The remaining 14 miles from Louth to Grimsby were straight and generally falling gently towards the north, the Wolds being kept to the west. In the run of four main stations were various halts put in to enliven the local runs. First came Fotherby and Utterby Halts before Ludborough at 5 miles from Louth (146m) which set the pattern for the others with a small yard, main building on the west side, parallel platforms and signal box on the east side controlling the level crossing. North Thoresby, 1m. 1,065yd. further on, was similar, with Grainby Halt and Holton Village north of it. Most of the villages mentioned are near the Grimsby-Louth road; Grainby Halt was delightfully odd in that it served a Victorian Hall and nothing else, some two miles west across the main road. The building stood empty for many years. The halt was a pretty one and had a natty single storey cabin.

Waltham is really the southern end of the suburbs of Grimsby, and New Waltham parish was in fact created in 1961. Both road and rail ran close together to serve the villages of Holton-le-Clay (150m) where the station was about one mile south of the village, being more useful for Tetney on the east side, and Waltham (152m), both stations in the same house style as the other two north of Louth. Waltham's platforms were staggered, the down being offset north of the up. On 11th September 1961 many stations in the area under review closed, among them were the halts, and on the whole of the 78 mile route from Peterborough, those left after that date were Spalding, Boston, Firsby, Burgh, Willoughby, Alford, Louth and North Thoresby. By the end, in 1970 only the two had survived. In its best imitation of the old Great Western, the GNR had two halts within the Grimsby town boundary, at Weelsby Road and Hainton Street, and shortly after, at 154½ miles Grimsby Goods Jc. was reached where the main route ended, forking left into Grimsby town station and right to Pasture Street signal box and the Cleethorpes direction.

North Thoresby stayed open as long as the final dmu service continued to run between Grimsby and Louth. Louth's C12s attended to the local workings, and coaches were fitted with retractable steps for serving the halts. The main line trains would often have the older GN types, including single wheelers, 2-4-0s and early 4-4-0s. 'Atlantics' were a rarity, though at the end of its days No. 2822 was to be seen at Grimsby. The GCR would bring up the King's Cross trains from Cleethorpes and the GN engine would be attached to the rear end for the run to Boston. In 1928 the Sentinel steam railcar 'Railway' was put into service between Grimsby and North Thoresby.

At Goods Jc. the GNR had control of three major functions in Grimsby; the electricity and gasworks and the refuse destructor, all of which were served by separate sidings from a rather compact layout. At the end of the right hand arm of the 'Y' the GN had its own goods warehouse off what had by then become a single line to run into the M & SL at Holme St. crossing. The left hand arm of the 'Y' curved round sharply to enter Grimsby Town station over Garden Street crossing. At the west end was Wellowgate crossing, and with Pasture Street adjacent to Holme Street, the distance table alone makes interesting reading. All the level crossings from the west have been included:

Littlefield crossing.
Friargate crossing. 227 yd.
Wellowgate crossing. 226 yd.
Garden St. crossing. 288 yd.
Pasture St. crossing. 466 yd.
Holme St. crossing. 72 yd.

It is possible that a good pair of lungs would have obviated the need for block instruments, especially in the last two cases!

Grimsby folk have long been patient and have tolerated frequent closures of the gates, often for trivial movements. Originally the idea was to build a new station north of Holme St. crossing which would have been easier for the GN who would have avoided reversal to their King's Cross trains. However, this was not to be and any other than seven coaches' length of train interfered with road traffic at each end. The station layout was neat, considering what little space was allowed. The main building was on the north side, and at the east end of the platform was a short parcels bay and docks for horses and carriages. The other platform was a central island linked by footbridge beneath the overall roof. The outer face was workable at both ends for each direction and two extra tracks here could be used as up and down loops. However, the outer platform 3 could just hold seven coaches without fouling all the connections in and out of the station on the south side. This No.3 platform was actually used by main line trains from Cleethorpes to the west, leaving No.2, the inner face, for GN arrivals which were often of nine bogies and would have an engine at each end for a short time while reversal took place. What must be emphasised here is that most of the fish traffic from the docks, all the excursion traffic and GN iron ore bound for Scunthorpe passed through the bottleneck and over all the level crossings.

Looking towards Cleethorpes, or Cleethorpe as it was originally, the branch to Grimsby Docks, opened in August 1852 went, along with an eastbound relief line, as far as New Bridge Sidings with malteries on the

A J63 causes gate closure at Garden St. crossing, Grimsby.   C. T. Goode

1930s view of return day excursions at Cleethorpes.   *Collection, C. T. Goode*

north side and the original locomotive depot on the south housing 18 engines in a six road terminal shed. Grimsby Docks station was a dull place, a single storey building with offices at the north end of the Doncaster platform,

Great Activity at Cleethorpes Road Jc. looking towards New Clee. The crossing here, once one of the busiest in the UK, is now replaced by a bridge. The lines straight ahead lead to the docks and GN warehouse; the main line curves right. The motive power visible is a D11 on a passenger train, and two B1s. Beneath the cabin a poster advertises Runabout tickets at 17/6 and 20/-.   *C. T. Goode*

B1 No. 61170 waits to leave Cleethorpes.   C. T. Goode

and a long waiting shed on the north side. As the line curved round to the east it passed over one of the busiest level crossings in the country, a wide affair on the skew beset by tram, later by trolleybus wires for vehicles linking Grimsby with Cleethorpes, manned by a policeman to see fair play. The cabin was Cleethorpe Road Jc., with Fish Dock Road crossing box for company hard by. The branch to Cleethorpes, opened only after protracted negotiations with local landowners on 6th April 1863, pursued its course along the estuary shore for 2½ miles before entering the station hard by the pier and Big Dipper. New Clee station was small, 1 m. 652 yd. from the terminus, the cabin here splitting up the long block section. After Suggitt's Lane crossing box, the terminus was reached, supervised by a large cabin on the seafront side. The layout has seen successive remodelling, though the number of platforms has remained at six. The original layout was probably the simplest in some respects, though a later revision gave access to all platforms for arrivals and departures. At one time, too, the main building was on the south side away from the sea and adjacent to platform 1. Later, however, the more usual arrangement of concourse and buildings at the buffer ends was adopted, and a small decorative tower was inserted. The final version was a modernisation of the buildings in a functional style in July 1961. Next to the signal box and hard by the promenade railings was a turn table and a stabling point for engines, and the line-up of handsome GC locomotives being attended to here proved a far bigger attraction to the juvenile railway man than did any donkey ride or amusement arcade! As well as the tourist, the station facilities catered for a 'better class' of clientele, as witnessed by the Private Parlour and Refreshments, and the First Class Ladies.

Running west in the opposite direction from Grimsby Town station through the three level crossings and past the triangular junction with the Grimsby District Light Railway at Marsh Jc., where the cabin was set boldly in the centre of things to cover the three intersections, the first station out was Great Coates, the first of the villages all served by the railway lying to the south along the A1136 road. Here was a simple yard layout on the south side east of the station, with the tickets issued from the stationmaster's house by the level crossing facing the village at the west end. A further mile and 550 yd.

further came Healing, again close to a large village which was, as might be suspected, named after curative spring hereabouts. The station actually materialised some time after the others on this route, and the original layout shows nine long sidings running parallel to the main line on the north side, an interesting feature which may have been put in for overflow storage of rolling stock brought out of Cleethorpes at the height of the season. These disappeared early on, leaving Healing much as Great Coates with the same basic layout, except that the signal box was at the south side of the line. Stallingborough, one mile west, was likewise endowed, with the addition of a cattle dock and with a village which spilled over to the north side of the level crossing. The main road to Immingham crossed the line on the skew at Little London, while further on was the cabin at Roxton Sidings, which was there to supervise an agricultural siding and the level crossing. For many years the eastbound up home signal was a GN somersault type, centrally pivotted and a stranger in the midst of GCR territory. Just as strange was Habrough Jc., 1½ miles further west where the lines to New Holland and Barnetby diverged. This parting of the ways was interesting in that the Barnetby line, which was junior to the other route by several years, came down parallel with it to Habrough level crossing, giving a deceptive four track stretch before being brought in as a normal junction. This was evidently done to save a further cabin at what would have been the point of junction. Later, in 1883 to save

Typical Habrough scene. Note the length of the train and fruit in boxes on the platform.
T. Rounthwaite

imposing speed restrictions on the express trains running to and from Barnetby on a line which had now become more important, a compromise was reached by the unusual step of turning both lines out on reverse curves instead of only the left hand one, a most interesting and somewhat eccentric achievement. Habrough's platforms were staggered on each side of the level crossing. There were also sidings on each side of the running lines, those on the north side having the cattle dock and warehouse. The small village lay north of the line and the station was perhaps more of a changing place; the westbound platform had a set of route indicator boards.

D9 No. 6024 at Habrough on a mixed collection of coaches. 4/8/1934.   T. Rounthwaite

Actually, the approved place at which to change was Ulceby, on the north side of the triangle of lines running to New Holland, for here were well appointed premises on both sides and where it was decided to open a refreshment room, though nothing came of it. Hard by, though, was the Yarborough Inn, itself adjacent by chance to a large piggery. Prior to April 1888 the main line was Manchester to New Holland, so that Ulceby was the point of change for Grimsby. Thereafter Brockleby, suitably upgraded in 1889, became the point at which passengers left the main line to Grimsby for New Holland. Off the curve from Habrough came four sidings for a warehouse, coal drops and cattle pens, while in the centre of the junction were pits from which ballast was taken. The signal box here was a tall one which ultimately controlled the junction for Immingham north of the platforms. Ulceby village is large and has a church with a twisting spire in the Chesterfield tradition, well to the west of the line.

Lincoln was the focal point of many lines, the huge boss of the wheel whose spokes radiated widely in all directions. As at Grimsby the GN station was beset by a level crossing at each end, though the restrictions were not quite so acute as there was room for manoeuvre in the station limits. Additionally there was the relief line to the south for trains not seeking the station, and the removal of Pelham Street crossing in later years, replaced by a bridge, though the complex junction remained.

The GN station had eight platforms, Nos.1-4 being bays at the east end, while Nos.5 and 6 were the main through ones. No.6 was an island with No.7 on the opposite to give additional westbound accommodation. The station building was constructed by Peto & Betts, the architect John Taylor, in grey brick in a mock Tudor style. Functionally it was an open station, that is, tickets were collected before passengers alighted, in this case at a ticket platform at the Holmes from which collectors would descend. Logical reductions took the rails away from Platform 8 and from some of the bays.

D16 No. 62524 at Lincoln shed.   *C. T. Goode*

   To describe in words the track arrangements at Lincoln would be virtually impossible, as there were copious yards on either side, especially at the west end with the 'Bog' sidings, Goods shed, cattle and coal depots all on the north side and a neat fan of five sidings for each direction on the south side backed by the four road loco. depot with its facilities including a 70ft. turntable and coaling plant. Even further south were more sidings whose outlets faced west. From the bottleneck of High Street level crossing and the swing bridge over Brayford Waterway the two running lines fanned out from East Holmes box to be generally collected up again at West Holmes, where a reverse loop went round to Boultham Jc. on the avoiding line.

C4 Atlantic No. 6087 at Lincoln shed.   *Collection, C. T. Goode*

Pelham Street Jc. at the east end had a busy time with its level crossing and the lines running off in four directions, to Barnetby, Boston, Sleaford and another reversing loop to the avoiding line.

To take the Barnetby line first: This passed the former GC shed of five roads on the right, closed originally, then refurbished to become the later diesel depot. On either side were the factories of Messrs Ruston & Hornsby, Clayton Dewandre and Jewson's timber yard before the Witham was crossed, bringing the line to the power station on the right with an adjacent forge. Monks Abbey signal box on the right hand side controlled the siding connections here, and there was also a refuge siding for 35 wagons on the up side.

Thereafter came a steady run of 3¼ miles to the first rural station of Reepham, situated in the village it served. Here were parallel platforms and a couple of goods sidings with the signal box on the east side. The next station, Langworth, was astride the A158 road to Louth with the Station Hotel at the level crossing opposite the signal box and with the platforms north of them both. Here was an ample goods yard on both sides, with the village itself well down the road to the east.

Snelland, just over 3 miles north, served a hamlet east of the line, but here was also a decent sized goods yard at the south end, with the signal box on the west side controlling the level crossing. Reasby Hall, a building dating back to 1708, overlooked the line before the station was reached. Around Wickenby (1 m. 928 yd.) there appears to have been nothing but woods, and it is one of these stations for which there seems to have been little excuse. The compact village, complete with thatch, lay a fair way off to the east, and the station had a simple goods yard on the same side, plus level crossing and signal box on the west side.

A fine chance was missed to award a station to the village of Buslingthorpe, near which the line passed over two level crossings. In the event it had a long run north east of almost four miles before reaching Market Rasen, a place of some substance with a racecourse and with Middle and West Rasen out on the Gainsborough road. The town is busy and is surrounded by woodland, with shelter offered by the eastern hills. The MS & L gave its station distinction by providing an overall roof and yards on both sides south of the site and on the east side north of the station. As expected there was a horse and cattle dock, and a large warehouse. For once there was no level crossing here and the signal box at the south end was left to get on with supervising the shunting. Pickup workings from West Holmes and Barnetby directions met here at around two o'clock daily.

North of Market Rasen the line turned due north to reach Claxby & Usselby station (2 m. 1,487 yd.), a simple place with signal box at the south end, level crossing and goods yard and building on the Usselby side, that is, the west. Claxby was on the other side and neither place was close to the railway. The station was situated on Usselby Moor. Short of the station was Stubbing's Sidings, to which access was gained from the down line, while beyond were the Mid Lincs. Ironstone Sidings reached from the up side. The former was somewhat vague, while the latter had a long reference to it in the Working Appendix. There were four more stations before the line from Lincoln reached the junction at Wrawby. Holton-le-Moor (2 m. 1,297 yd.) was on the A46, set on the skew and on the wrong side of a park away from the village to be effective, though a large goods yard was here on the east side. Moortown

(1m. 1,137yd.) lay at the east end of the village and was unusual in that the premises were on the wrong side, away from the population served, and also in that the goods yard had a long spur on the east side needing a ground frame to work the outlet points at the north end. North Kelsey (1m. 789yd.) was a good two miles away to the east of this large village, though in a cluster of premises on the east side was the Queen's Head Hotel. Goods accommodation on the west side was primitive, and the platforms were south of the level crossing. Last of all was Howsham (1m. 1,452yd.) in a most isolated position, the village lying to the west. The station was unusual for this route in having staggered platforms, each side of the level crossing with the small yard opposite the up platform on the east side. Wrawby Jc. was reached just over 3½ miles beyond, the convergence being the right hand of the three.

Departures at Market Rasen in 1949 were as follows:

To Cleethorpes from Lincoln 6.06a.m., 9.08, 10.13SO ex Leicester, 1.31p.m.XP, 5.41, 8.21XP from Birmingham , 4.45., and 9.21.

and the reverse direction: 7.59a.m.XP to Birmingham, 8.19, 9.53XP, 1.26p.m., 2.24SO to Leicester, 3.46, 6.55.
There was no Sunday service.

Lincolnshire begins in a remote north west corner where Thorne is left behind and the dull, flat and very agricultural levels of Hatfield Chase are to be found. For a few miles the old South Yorkshire Railway ran east through the last remaining stretches of Yorkshire alongside the Stainforth & Keadby canal, through Medge Hall station, still in Yorkshire but Lincolnshire in spirit. Here was a station devoid of all but a small building, one siding, level crossing and waterways on each side, with a road swing bridge over the canal. Over the border in Lincs. the first stop was Godknow Bridge, perhaps really Godforsaken as the site had simply its platforms, stationmaster's house, crossing and swing bridge, but no pointwork and no habitation around it. For many years the station had been closed to passengers. From these humble beginnings the line could only progress to better things, which it did by arriving at Crowle, 2½ miles from Medge Hall, called Central during most of its life because of the presence of the Axholme Joint Railway station in the village. This did in fact get close to the centre of things, as the 'Central' station lay over a mile to the south. However, it had several watercourses for company and the approach from the north brought one first to the South Yorkshire Hotel, then the booking office and waiting room on the left, after which one had to cross the Keadby canal to find the platforms east of the level crossing. There was a large goods yard north of the line at the east end reached by a long connection across the water. Here too were up and down refuge sidings for 50 wagons.

East of the station in later days the line was crossed at right angles by the AJR on a long viaduct taking in the railway and three watercourses. Beyond Crowle the railway history and topography becomes more complicated, due to the extension of the SYR line over the Trent and also to the renewal of the bridge across it. Originally the SYR ran straight to a terminal layout at Keadby near the locks where the canal met the Trent, where there were three coal shoots, cattle sidings and a small loco. depot of one road. The largest commercial premises was the South Yorkshire Hotel.

With opening of the line across the river, a junction was put in called Canal Jc., originally with an usual round cabin on the south side. A turntable was also provided to service the locos. on arrival. Where the canal was crossed by the new line a separate signal box was provided a short distance from the junction to work the swing bridge needed here. In later years Canal Jc. (2¾ miles) had refuge capacity for 55 wagons on the up side and 160 on the down.

Stations were provided for traffic on either side of the original swing bridge, namely Keadby & Althorpe to the west, a simple affair with level crossing and crossover at the east end and staggered platforms, and Gunness & Burringham to the east. These two places formed a long ribbon development along the road skirting the river and the station lay between the two. It had parallel platforms and several sidings on the north side, four of which ended over the river as coal shoots. The station building was on the towpath on the opposite side of the road to the station proper! The swing bridge would have its own cabin adjacent. On the opening of the lift bridge, a station was built just to the west of it, Althorpe, for Keadby, Gunness & Burringham (Keadby was the most obvious village). The station was a functional affair finished in best GCR green. The bridge was controlled from a cabin at the hinged end on the north side, and the run-up on each side was signalled by three position arms whose most memorable feature was the slow and leisurely way in which they changed aspects. The remains of the old layout were brought in at Gunhouse Jc. (1 m.) before the line ran over the Scotter Road viaduct to enter the area of Scunthorpe & Frodingham station (2m.). This was of course the later building set to the south of the town which had grown rapidly and where the development of the railway had been equally spectacular. Originally there had been a station, Frodingham, to the east of the later one, set under the eye of the Midland Ironstone Company signal box on the south side, two platforms east of a level crossing with a simple building on the north side. South of the site were the Frodingham Ironworks with its four retorts prominently seen, while to the east were the Lindsey Ironworks whose sidings, and others, were controlled by Trent Ironworks cabin on the south

Scunthorpe Station.

British Rail

side. At the east end of the industrial complex was the North Lincoln signal box which controlled yard on both sides and spurs to Dawes Siding (north) and Beal's Siding (south). Subsequent developments demanded no fewer than six cabins, that at Trent Jc. being the busiest. Passing beneath the Ashby road bridge the layout opened out into a set of 24 sidings on the south side with a coal yard and loading docks at the extreme edge. The station and signal cabin were to the north, the former with parallel platforms and a bay at the Grimsby end. East of here the later NLLR took off to the north and opportunity was taken to form a generous triangular junction in which were set a goods depot and the adjacent Frodingham loco. depot, a through shed of five roads. Frodingham and its industrial life lay to the south of the main line, served by a network of goods lines, some which were privately owned. Running north from the top of the triangle the NLLR served further steelworks on both sides with signal boxes at Crosby Mines and Normanby Park South and North.

The Working Appendix carried a special reference to this spot:

'When the Midland Ironstone Company require to perform operations on their property within a distance of 200 yards from the NLLR between Crosby Mines and Normanby Park South signal boxes, the Signalman at Crosby Mines will be advised by the Firm's staff. It will then be necessary for arrangements to be made for no train or engine to be within 200yd. of the site of the blasting throughout the time this is being performed. Should the section at the time notice is given by the Firm be occupied by any train or engine, the Firm's staff must be requested not to commence blasting until the train or engine has been removed to a distance of not less than 200yd. from the site, and steps must be taken to carry out the removal as quickly as possible.'.

Some ideas of the extent of local traffic generated in the area may be given by listing the pilot locomotives required from Frodingham shed to perform various duties in 1948:

Frodingham Trent Jc.	No.1	Marshalling	10p.m. Sunday	to 6p.m.	Sunday
New Yard Outside	No.2	Marshalling	10p.m. Sunday	to 6p.m.	Sunday
Works entrance 'A'	No.3	Marshalling	10p.m. Sunday	to 6p.m.	Sunday
North Lincoln	No.4	Marshalling	10p.m. Sunday	to 6p.m.	Sunday
Goods Yard	No.5	Marshalling	6a.m. to 10p.m. Weekdays		
Trent Down Sidings	No.6	Marshalling	10p.m. Sunday	to 6p.m.	Sunday
New Yard Inwards	No.7	Marshalling	6a.m. Monday	to 6p.m.	Sunday
Transfers	No.8	Transfers	10p.m. Sunday	to 6p.m.	Sunday
North Lincoln	No.9	Marshalling	3p.m. to 7a.m. Mon. to Fri.		
			3p.m. to 11p.m. Saturday		
Works Entrance 'E'	No.10	Marshalling	10p.m. Sunday	to 6p.m.	Sunday

Frodingham shed opened in 1914 and lasted as 36C until 22nd February 1966 with one WD 2-8-0 locomotive in final possession of a ramshackle building. Thirty works were listed as having rail access in the Scunthorpe area in 1930. At the east end of the industrial complex, mostly to do with iron and steel, was the Santon Brickworks served by a siding from the signal box of that name.

Throughout its vigorous industrial life, Scunthorpe had great rapport with the railways which fed it with iron ore from Immingham and High Dyke in the Midlands, and supplied it with coal from both directions, east and west. Its finished products also went by rail and the inadequate roads had little of this traffic to bear. In the Indian summer, before recession hit the area a £69 million scheme was completed by British Steel for a new coke oven and coal handling plant on the up side of the lines near Trent Jc. to handle all the fuel for the area. A new rod and coil mill was built in 1976 at a cost of £35 million to increase production of the items alongside the existing plant, for which specially adapted wagons were made. At Normanby Park expansion to the tune of £47 million was indulged in, to improve the output of steel billets by a further two thirds by 1978. The last major drive by BR to meet this expansion was the starting of what was called the Steelink service between Scunthorpe and Wolverhampton. This was to move up to 600 tonnes daily in one train which left early each day, the first leaving at 10.30 a.m. on a day in November 1980 and arriving in Wolverhampton at 2.30 p.m. The claim was made at the time of launching that 50% of Black Country steel was moved by rail.

Once clear of chimneys and smoke the NLLR pursued a rural course to the Humber along a single line worked by electric train staff from Normanby Park North to Winteringham station (2¼). Between lay halts at Winterton & Thealby and West Halton where ground frames were situated, to control Sir Berkeley Sheffield's Siding and the Bagmoor Siding. At Winteringham the line turned east round the north end of the village and ran into three terminal sidings, one of which had a passenger platform on its northern side. The line continued short of these, turning north to run to the water's edge at the Haven where there was a run-round loop and siding. Again the single line set off again, short of the buffer stops and turning west this time running almost three miles to Whitton, where there was a crude layout of single platform with building and a run-round line plus siding and weigh bridge.

RCTS Special at West Halton. 20/6/54.   *C. T. Goode*

The 1914 passenger service for the line was:

Scunthorpe	7.35a.m.	1.20p.m.	6.20	
Whitton	8.10	1.55	6.44	
Whitton	8.15	2.00	6.50	
Scunthorpe	8.50	2.35	7.15	Weekdays Only

After 1922 there was one train each way on weekdays, this withdrawn on 13th July 1925. Freight movements continued to be heavy, but these were cut back successively from Winteringham & Whitton from 1st October 1951, West Halton 29th May 1961 and Winterton & Thealby 20th July 1964. In 1948 the one pickup left Frodingham Yard at 9 a.m., arriving Whitton at 11.30, apparently staying there until 4.40 p.m. and getting back to base at 6.35 p.m.

Returning now to the main line. The course followed from Santon was generally eastern, though somewhat sinuous to Appleby station (1¾m.) suffixed 'Lincs' to avoid confusion with the two other stations serving the famous town on the edge of the Lake District. The site was a pleasant one lying on the north-south line of Roman Ermine Street and with woods to the south. The village lay a good mile north. Charles Winn had an ironstone siding here in the early days on the village side, but this vanished long ago, leaving the small goods yard opposite. Platforms were staggered here, though not on each side of the level crossing. Both were east of this and a refuge siding lay on the north side, later removed when a similar facility for each direction was provided at Elsham (4¾m.) which was not to be outdone, lying on the A15 from Brigg. The village lay 1½ miles away and beyond Elsham Hall, home of the Elwes family. Elsham station was virtually a mirror image of Appleby, having the same sort of platform arrangement, this time west of the road. To split up the long block section Worlaby Siding signal box existed, about equidistant between the two stations.

Barnetby West signal box, wholly of wood and the first of three huge cabins to disappear.   *C. T. Goode*

A B1 enters Barnetby on a stopping train. The East signal box is visible.   C. T. Goode

After passing beneath the A18 and, latterly, the new M18, the line ran for two miles to reach Wrawby Jc. which it gained by a rather sharp curve, the Brigg line having the best of the three approaches here.

The section between Wrawby Jc. and Brocklesby was widened basically to four tracks under the Act of 1912 to cater for the increase in traffic expected from the opening of Immingham Dock, and the general economic buoyancy of the time. Wrawby Jc. cabin on the north side was most impressive, open continuously and requiring two men and a lad to operate its many levers and to book the trains during its heyday. In the fork of the Lincoln and Retford lines was a two road engine shed with turntable to cater for traffic using the

Tudor Twists at Brocklesby station.   *C. T. Goode*

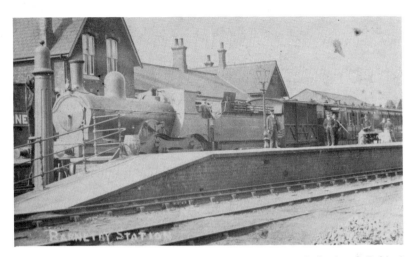

A rare pre-widening scene at Barnetby.   *Collection, C. T. Goode*

sidings set on both sides of the line. Two tall wooden signal cabins, West and East, dealt with the movements around Barnetby station where the block working between the cabins must have been a fascinating study. Barnetby station itself saw great changes when the original building of standard Conisbrough pattern was removed and a Stainforth type of layout with double island arrangements to serve the four tracks was installed. A footbridge linked it all to the building which lay away to the north of the layout opposite the Station Hotel (Proprieter Joseph Smissons). If the refreshment here proved too potent, then there was a Temperance Hotel adjacent to the stationmaster's house itself, well away from the action in King's road. Could this have been the refreshment room offered here in GC days? Behind Barnetby East on the south side was a large cattle and sheep market with a loading dock across the Victoria road. Opposite the signal box was a very large malthouse. In the days of wooden wagons with grease axles boxes the services of the repairers, the Lincoln Wagon & Engine Co. and Messrs. T. Burnett on site at the station would have been welcome. Chalk quarries 2½ miles to the east were given rail connection controlled by Melton Ross Sidings signal box, and some five miles east of Barnetby, Brocklesby station was reached, the junction where the line divided northwards to Ulceby and New Holland, and round the base of the triangle layout towards Habrough Jc.

The station building at Brocklesby with its Tudor twisted chimneys survived the rebuilding of 1912 virtually in the same form which Prince Albert had known when the line was opened. Chief alterations were the provision of a bridge instead of a level crossing and the directing of the extra running lines round the outside of the existing platform layout. The up side became an island and there remained only the one platform for the Barnetby direction. Passenger traffic was never very heavy here and the station was built to serve Brocklesby Hall. The nearest village was Ulceby which had its own station to the north.

The line north of Ulceby station struck out north east for the run of almost four miles to the Immingham Reception Sidings. With the cessation of passenger trains thereon it was worked on the permissive block. From the

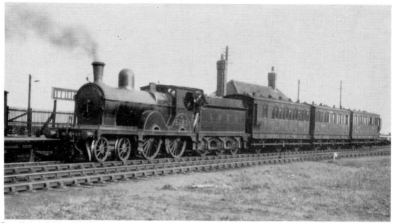

Small 4-4-0 No. 5683 at Immingham Dock.   *T. Rounthwaite*

West Jc. at Immingham the line ran back to Goxhill (see below), was single and worked on the electric tablet system. Immingham Dock station was by the Entrance Lock and was a single storey structure with two high chimneys. An old coach served to house the 'usual offices'. The run from the single platform at Immingham Dock was just over seven miles to Goxhill, first round the Export Dock and then to halts at Killingholme, Admiralty Platform and East Halton used by the five or six trains which ran to and from New Holland. In 1949 the service was as follows:

Immingham Dock	7.43a.m.	12p.m.SO	12.10SX	2.45	5.15	7.05FSX
New Holland	8.18	12.35	12.40	3.15	5.44	7.35
New Holland	6.40	8.50	1.45	4.00		6.17FSX
Immingham Dock	7.10	9.20	2.15	4.30		6.47

No. 5683 sorts through some freight at Barton-on-Humber.   *T. Rounthwaite*

C12 No. 4019 gets attention at New Holland Pier in 1932.   *T. Rounthwaite*

A Sentinel locomotive ran from Immingham loco. depot at 12.15p.m. to New Holland Town, arriving 1.13 p.m. on Saturdays. The return working left at 1.30 p.m. arriving at Immingham at 2.28 p.m. This was probably the time when engines were changed over; two Sentinels were allocated to New Holland shed.

Travelling towards New Holland from Ulceby there were two stations encountered, the first being Thornton Abbey (2½m.) which had two small signal boxes at West and East controlling level crossings until the road to Thornton Abbey ruins was demoted to a footpath in 1885 and a new link was put in passing the station to Barton road. Latterly the remaining signal box was closed and a ground frame provided to operate the siding and crossover. There were parallel platforms, simple buildings including an iron gents' urinal

D9 No. 6024 marshalls a horse box on to some decidedly vintage rolling stock on the New Holland triangle.   *T. Rounthwaite*

as the only adornment on the down side, and huge name boards. Thornton Curtis village lay a good way to the west. Goxhill (4¼m.) was however in its village and had a straight forward station layout with coal and cattle siding. The later addition, the line from Immingham Dock, came in under the eye of the signal box south of the level crossing, and latterly all the signals here were of GCR vintage. The old brass bell used to announce trains was also to be found.

Arriving in the vicinity of New Holland, first met with was Oxmarsh Jc, signal cabin and level crossing, (1,461yd.). The early plans gave a signal box on each side of the line here. The main route actually kept straight on to run east of the timber dock to an outer basin and Earles' shipyard, while the passenger lines curved westwards to Barrow Road signal box at one corner of a triangular layout which led west towards the Barton line and north into New Holland Town station. On the southern curve of the triangle was the engine shed, a through one of four roads with Barton Jc. signal box at the west corner and New Holland Town signal box at the north corner. In the centre of the triangle was a reservoir, presumably for engine water. Between the abovementioned docks and the passenger station were sidings for the handling of coal, which had increased over the years from six to ten in number. Land to the south of the engine shed in New Holland village was given over to the Yarborough Hotel, artisans' cottages set round a quadrangle in Manchester Square, churches and a school and the laundry which was closed in 1931. A reading room here was financed by the fines collected from staff for swearing at places of employment east of Retford - elsewhere on the MS & L their oaths kept a similar establishment at Gorton in newspapers and such! West of New Holland station the land was earmarked for repair shops for the ferryboats and the landing stages, and jetties. New Holland Town station had four lines through it and had at first an overall roof. At various

K3 2-6-0 No. 61852 waiting with a Cleethorpes train at New Holland Town.   A. J. Wickens

70

times there were cutbacks here and there, but in its final form it retained its solid building with various offices, though not its refreshment room, and a fine set of GCR signals. The extension out on to the pier was executed in double track having a cartway on the west side and a walkway for passengers on the east. This gave an apparent extension of the platforms to the Pier station which had a platform on each side of the running lines and a central road which held coal wagons for the steamers. The layout changed here slightly over the years, being made smarter with a scissors crossover and furnished with a cabin and levers which was only considered as a ground frame. The absolute end was marked as 107m. 1 furlong and 70 chains from Manchester, and it was strange at times to see an old GC passenger engine standing by the stops on an arrival with its buffers virtually poised over the river.

To gain the Barton branch the triangle was rejoined at Town station and the single line staff received by the train at Barton Jc. box, or in later years at New Holland Town. The single line ran due west for 3½ miles to Barton, passing on the way the simple halt of Barrow Haven. Here there was a decidedly rude waiting shed, a stationmaster's house and both road and watercourse crossings. The nearest neighbour was a brickworks, while Barrow village lay some two miles inland. Barton station was quite busy for its size and had everything needed within an economical layout. On the north side of the single platform, beyond which was the town, was a large set of coal drops which were removed quite early, in June 1886, and the main building with awning which faced the run-round loop, a goods shed and malt kiln, also a bone mill set at right angles to the lines so as to be parallel to the creek which came up from the Humber at that point. The layout was completed by a long siding running round towards the river on which was a cattle landing. There seems to have been only a ground frame at this location. Immingham shed sent down some remarkably large engines on the branch passenger trains, looking uncomfortable tender first.

Only the GC section would perhaps have the sense of humour to put one of their best engines, here C5 No. 5365 "Sir William Pollitt" on a tender-first job of 6 wheelers at Barton-on-Humber!   *T. Rounthwaite*

The Working Appendix gave the following note on Barton:

'When it is necessary for a freight train or light engine to run from New Holland to Barton-on-Humber whilst vehicles occupy the platform at Barton, New Holland must be advised and the enginemen must be notified at the time the train staff is handed to them at New Holland that vehicles are in the platform line. In such circumstances the driver must stop at the ground frame situated 90 yd. east of Barton station. The stationmaster at Barton must arrange for a man, with the necessary hand signals, to be posted at the ground frame and exhibit a danger signal on all occasions when such conditions apply to ensure the driver stopping. During fog or falling snow the Hand-signalman must, in addition, place a detonator on the line'.

New Holland was a most inhospitable place, cold even in high summer. A local sufferer wrote to the 'Hull Daily Mail': 'I invite New Holland residents to compare the reception they receive in Hull with that afforded to visitors to New Holland. There is not the slightest doubt that in the past many people have been put off visiting New Holland. The bus, allegedly run in conjunction with the ferry, is waiting at New Holland Town station where it stays with closed doors until the scheduled departure time of 11.45 a.m. or later. The bus terminus is the car park; there is nowhere for passengers to sit except the rather dismal railway station waiting room, and there are no refreshment facilities. I suggest that a notice to visitors to take the next ferry back to Hull would be a gesture of honesty.' (Mr. B. Pugh.).

In 1981 New Holland began to feel the impact of the new Humber Bridge when, after closure of the ferry, it lost its bus service and became reliant on its admittedly superior hourly service of dmus between Barton and Cleethorpes via the remaining south curve at New Holland. In 1976 BR sought to stop running the Sunday services on the line and Humberside County Council granted £2,000 to keep these running. A survey showed that up to 250 people travelled to and from New Holland.

Barton Branch service 1949.

Barton	6.15a.m.	6.50	7.50	9.44	11.35	12.30p.m.	1.25
New Holland Pr.	6.26	7.01	8.03	9.56	11.48	12.42	1.37
New Holland Pr.	6.34	7.13	8.55	10.50	12.00SO	12.40SX	12.50SO
Barton	6.45	7.25	9.07	11.05 **	12.12	12.52	1.02

					ThSO		
Barton	3.10	5.37	7.30	8.53	10.10		
New Holland Pr.	3.22	5.46	7.42	9.05	10.22	ThSO	
New Holland Pr.	2.05	4.05	6.00	7.56	9.20	11.08	
Barton	2.17	4.17	6.12	8.09	9.33	11.19	

** Mixed train. 5.37p.m. ex Barton terminates at Town stn.

Striking eastwards from Lincoln towards Boston, a line left the Barnetby line at Pelham Street crossing and the Sleaford line at Sincil Bank, passing behind the carriage sidings which became the revitalised loco. depot. Beyond the sewage beds the line picked up the river Witham on its left at Washingboro Jc. - (2m. 88yd.). Some three miles further on the rather isolated station of Five Mile House was reached with its potato and sugar beet siding. The latter commodity was handled intensively at Bardney Jc. a good two miles further on, where the crop, essentially seasonal, demanded special trains which were worked latterly by Class 31 and 47 diesel engines as required. Bardney station was rather a jolly affair with an Italianate tower on the north side of the line at the end of the village. The Louth branch came in trailing from the north at West signal box, and ran into the main side platform which had all the offices on it. The main lines ran alongside and had their own island between them with the Station cabin at the east end, giving a most unusual layout, though it did leave the Louth trains completely independent of the main lines whose trains could neither run on or off the branch directly. On the north side of the station was a large goods yard, a branch run-round, and turntable, while on the south side was a refuge siding for 64 wagons.

The Louth branch set off north east, keeping Bardney well to the east, then running generally north through Kingthorpe to the village of Wragby on the west side of the line, the station at almost six miles from the terminus. Here was a simple platform, level crossing, passing loop and a couple of sidings on the east side. The single line continued in a north east direction through East Barkwith (2¾m.) to South Willingham where the next passing loop was located. Hereafter the line braced itself to cross the Wolds, turning east and running through South Willingham tunnel (557yd.) before reaching Donington-on-Bain station and passing loop (3m.), the village some way back to the north and close by the Belmont TV transmitter. To maintain a reasonable level the line twisted somewhat, but eventually took a north east direction to enter the second tunnel of Withcall (971yd.). Withcall station followed at 3m. 176yd. from Donington, a typically isolated place at a level crossing. The last station before Louth South signal box was reached was Hallington, 1¾m. from Withcall and three miles from the end of the branch. The steepest gradient on the branch was 1 in 70.

Bardney Branch trains 1879. Weekdays Only.

	a.m.		p.m.	
Louth	8.05	10.29	2.56	5.40
Bardney	8.54	11.29	3.47	6.30
Bardney	9.10	11.00	4.26	7.00
Louth	10.01	11.56	5.16	7.55

and in 1949:

	a.m.	p.m.			a.m.
Louth	7.48	12.40	3.57	Pickup Goods	8.05
Bardney	8.36	1.29	4.46		11.13
Bardney	9.55	1.50	6.25		12.05
Louth	10.41	2.37	7.13		3.20

The pickup took any Kingthorpe wagons to Wragby and returned with them next day. The engine shunted the yard at Wragby and the 1.50 p.m. ex Bardney passed it at Donington-on-Bain. The line closed on 5th November 1951 and was closed completely from Donington to Louth on 17th September 1956.

From Bardney the Boston line ran a little more south than east, keeping the Witham on its right hand to reach Southrey (2m. 998yd.) and Stixwould (1m.

73

1,063yd.). The first station had its village north and adjacent, while the latter took its clientele from two miles away. The station was small, wooden and isolated here, and both were able to survive due to weekend angling parties which sallied forth in groups from places like Wadsley Bridge. A further 2¼ miles was Woodhall Jc., a place remarkably similar to Bardney in a confusing sort of way, as the buildings were of the same proportions and in the same place; the sidings, too, were at the same end. Here, however, the resemblance ended as there were two main platforms, that at the south side bearing a fine cast iron gents' urinal. Adjacent to the up platform was a bay for the Horncastle branch trains which sported a length of awning. A curiosity here was that the branch working had to be propelled out of the platform and then reversed to run rightaway on the branch which curved in facing the Boston direction. This was originally done to enable through workings from King's Cross to run directly to Horncastle and the original station, once called Kirkstead, was left beyond the point of divergence. Kirkstead was a fishermen's inn and a handful of cottages on the wrong side of the river. Woodhall Spa was 1½ miles along the branch and by a straight road from the junction. The 7½ mile line was more or less a direct run north east and remained nominally independent until 1923. It was worked on the staff and ticket system and there was a passing loop-cum-siding and skew level crossing south east of the little town which had been a spa for about 160 years. The run was a steady climb of three miles through pleasant woodland and heath, then falling along the Horncastle canal and river Bain to reach the terminus which was out to the west on the A158 road to Wragby.

The buildings at Horncastle were substantial, of brick of which about 50% towards the buffers was of rather domestic two storey appearance with five upper windows and a house roof with drooped ends. An awning of the Firsby type covered part of the single platform, supported by iron pillars on the offside. A short bay was to be found out in the open, capable of holding three 6 wheelers. There was a fair goods yard on the east side, plus a small engine shed probably for a single locomotive. The signal box was opposite on the west side and supervised a turn-in to a line parallel to the platform line, used for running round and giving access to a cattle dock, malthouse and warehouse. One interesting feature was a goods shed at right angles to the line next to the station building, reached by a wagon turntable between the platform end and the final buffers. Horncastle signal box was 5 miles 1,448yd. from Woodhall Spa.

Basic operations on the branch catered for five passenger trains each way and one round pickup trip. A Boston engine covered the morning workings, leaving there at 6.25a.m. for Woodhall Jc. with Horncastle parcels. It left Woodhall Jc. at 7.15 and after two round trips was back in Boston at 10.24. A Lincoln engine left the city at 7.00a.m. to Woodhall Jc. yard, leaving there at 9.35 for Horncastle on the Goods (maximum 38 wagons). It returned as a mixed train of passengers and goods at 12.42p.m. to Woodhall Jc. Two further round trips followed, the last getting back to Horncastle at 5.04p.m. After a breather the engine set off for home with the 6p.m. Goods to Lincoln. The last passenger working was a straight out and home run, dep. Boston 6.45p.m., reverse Woodhall Jc. and a ten minute turn round in Horncastle, getting back to Boston at 8.52p.m. These times reflect 1950s practice.

The through workings belong largely to the pre 1914 period, when a King's Cross-Horncastle coach was attached to the 4p.m. Leeds and transferred at

Peterborough. Later the coach ran as far as Boston as part of the 4.05p.m. Down Cleethorpes, the reverse arrangements remaining the same.

Marking the southern edge of this survey of Lincolnshire railways was the cut-off line opened on 1st July 1913 between Coningsby Jc. at 1m. 600yd. from Woodhall Jc., and Bellwater Jc. on the East Lincs. line. This ran for fifteen miles and was used chiefly for coastal excursion traffic which had hitherto to traipse into Boston and out again. On the double line there were stations at Coningsby, almost three miles from the junction and set in the village on the east side of the main road. The line then ran due eastwards for a further 2½ miles to the quaintly named Tumby Woodside station, situated rather remotely in the flat lands near farms called No Man's Friend and a road junction with a unique signpost pointing to New York one way and Boston the other. Tumby Woodside was a straggle of properties south of the station, while Tumby proper was some three miles away. The station had parallel platforms and brick waiting rooms on each side, while the single storey booking office was quite separate and by the road on the north side of the level crossing. New Bolingbroke (2¼m.) was equally remote and its extended village was north of the line. Here was a refuge siding for 54 wagons on the up side. Proceeding due east over the West Fen the line came next to Stickney, a substantial village south of the line on the A16 to Grimsby. The station (2¼m.) lay to the west of the road. Midville (2½m.) the last station before Bellwater Jc. would find it difficult to justify its existence except as a divider of a long block section. The location was completely isolated, seven feet above sea level crossing the Hobhole Drain and a minor road, with a chapel and inn for company. Only one train stopped here in 1914, that in the Skegness direction. Not so far away to the east was East Ville village with its station on the main line.

K2. No. 61757 shunts at Skegness 25/4/54.   *H. C. Casserley*

In addition to three weekdays only trains each way there were ten summer Saturday excursions which ran each way, eight serving Skegness, the rest Mablethorpe. The stations of origin were Basford & Bulwell, Kirkby-in-Ashfield, Chesterfield Central, Sheffield Vic., Bradford, Leeds and both Manchester London Road and Central. One train of special interest was the late 10.30p.m. departure from Lincoln to Coningsby on Saturdays and Sundays for RAF personnel. This called at Bardney and Woodhall Jc. and returned to Lincoln empty stock.

Returning to the junction at Firsby, one could find the branch to Spilsby which ran for four miles to a terminus situated just south of the little town. There was one intermediate station at Halton Holgate (2m.) which served the straggling village, sometimes spelt 'Holegate', to the north of the line. Originally there was an impressive service of passenger trains on the single line, but things were too ambitious and the line was reduced to one engine in steam and left to coal and oil traffic after 11th September 1939.

Services in 1914;

	a.m.					p.m.			
Firsby	7.10	8.47	10.10	11.25	12.50	4.25	6.16	6.50	7.35
Halton Holgate	7.19	8.53	10.16	11.34	12.56	4.34	6.22	6.56	7.41
Spilsby	7.24	8.58	10.21	11.39	1.01	4.39	6.27	7.01	7.46
Spilsby	6.40	8.15	9.50	10.35	12.25	3.30	5.50	6.35	7.15
Halton Holgate	6.44	8.19	9.54	10.39	12.29	3.36	5.56	6.39	
Firsby	6.50	8.25	10.00	10.45	12.35	3.44	6.04	6.45	7.24

It is evident that there must have been an engine kept at Spilsby to work the trains out and home. In 1950 the position had changed remarkably. The first trip out of Firsby was at 8.45a.m. leaving Spilsby again at 9.00. The only other trip was the 12.30p.m. out of Firsby, leaving Spilsby at 2.40p.m. and getting back to base at 2.55. The line was closed on 1st December 1958.

Taking now the lines running out of Lincoln westwards, the main route passed over High Street crossing, always busy, and the Holmes marshalling yards. The West goods yard was opened by the GCR on 8th September 1907, covered 70 acres and included the large warehouse. The later loco. depot, opened on closure of the one east of Pelham Street crossing, was to be found on the south side of the line, while the GER had its own shed at Pyewipe Jc. until 19th August 1925. The 1936 GCR shed complement was as follows:

Class K3 2-6-0 No. 135, Class K2 2-6-0 4673/53/33, Class D2 4-4-0 4303/20/76, Class D3 4-4-0 4309, Class B4 4-6-0 6013 6096, Class B5 4-6-0 5185 6072, Class B7 5478, Class J11 0-6-0 5177 6005, Class J67 0-6-0T 7396 7192 7377.

In 1980 there was a large diesel depot east of the station and only four locomotives-all else were units-were allocated there; 03 shunters Nos. 026, 034, 149 and 389. Two of these were outstationed at Boston.

Ex GE tank No. 8553 shunts while a GN freight passes Pyewipe Jc. on 19/4/47.

H. C. Casserley

At Pyewipe Jc. the GN & GE avoiding line came in from the south east, and there was also a reverse curve bringing traffic round to the east. Pyewipe Jc. signal box was on the south side and was busy; here too the old LD & ECR line to Chestefield diverged to the left. Country was soon reached thereafter and the line headed north east alongside the river Till towards Saxilby station, passing the Rowlands and Kesteven Sidings cabins serving peat works.

Architecture on the GN & GE Joint line at Haxey Jc. 18/9/71.   *T. G. Flinders*   77

From the latter box and level crossing to Saxilby station was exactly one mile. Saxilby station was in the village and both the cabin controlling the level crossing and the buildings were on the north side. A good 1½ miles further on came Sykes Jc., a remote cabin in the GER style on the left where the Clarborough-Retford line went off. The Up main distant here was unusually tall. The line ran through flat country but managed to hill and dale on 1 in 400 gradients, falling at such to Stow Park before a steady three mile pull at 1 in 200 to Lea. Stow Park could have been called after nearby Marton, in fact the buildings faced west towards that village; possibly the name was too common to adopt. Stow itself was 2½ miles away to the east. Shortly before Stow Park were WD fuel tanks served by sidings on the down side. On this side there were refuge facilities for 154 wagons, showing the traffic potential of the line. With a choice of three sites, the most southerly and worst was chosen for Lea station (2¾ miles), incidentally one of the shortest of names. The village lay to the west, the station situated in a modest cutting with an overbridge by way of a change.

After a level stretch the line fell at 1 in 400 to Gainsborough Lea Road station (2m. 355yd.), a fine spot with a handsome building in pale brick down off the embankment. Access to the platforms was by a wooden covered staircase, and on the up side was one of the two signal boxes here, latterly the only one. The other lay on the down side round the curve leading to the Trent Junctions with the GC line. There was a busy little yard here, doing quite a trade in oil products.

The Joint line continued through Nottinghamshire to Doncaster beyond the river crossing.

Operations on the Joint line were of unusual interest over a route which was quite lengthy on the run from London to Doncaster compared with the East Coast Main line. The GER obtained running powers from the NER in 1892 to run to York and ran for a time throughout from Liverpool Street via Doncaster. Then there were the services from March, three of them before 1914, of which the 6.42p.m. was heavily loaded with fruit traffic in season. There were corresponding up trains from Doncaster. In 1951 there was the 12.07p.m. Newcastle-Harwich Town, leaving Doncaster at 3.45p.m. via Gainsborough and Lincoln with a connection reaching Liverpool St. at 10p.m. This was followed by the glorious all-stations train out of Doncaster at 4.50p.m. which reached March at 9.02p.m. and giving an arrival in Liverpool St. at 2.28 a.m.!

After 1928 a train left Doncaster at 5.22p.m. for Liverpool St. which was sometimes started back from York, and there was also a Sunday train at 2.35p.m. which ran right up to 1939.

There was a named train on the Joint Line. This was the 'North Country Continental' from Harwich to York which, prior to 1914, shed a Liverpool portion at Lincoln to be taken forward by the GC via Sykes Jc. and Retford. After 1918 the main train ran to Liverpool and the York portion was detached at Lincoln. When they came along, B17 4-6-0s were used on the service, Gorton and Ipswich engines working outward alternately on odd days and providing a record as the longest through working by an engine on a cross-country train. After 1945 the engine and restaurant car were removed at Sheffield Vic. to wait for the service to return from Manchester. Latterly, this was the 8a.m. Parkeston Quay-Liverpool, a nine coach formation with restaurant car set front outward and rear on return.

The running times between Lincoln and Gainsborough were 23 minutes for the 15¾ miles and for the 21 miles to Doncaster were 27 minutes. Certain excursions from Leeds and Bradford ran non-stop to Lincoln via Doncaster, and those from Sheffield or Manchester went via Sykes Jc. Some halted at Lincoln for watering and crew changing, the engine, perhaps a Copley Hill B1, running through.

To the passenger workings can be added the horse box specials worked by K3s, B1s or B17s, and the newpaper and parcel trains. York B16s and V2s were to be found penetrating south on through workings in reciprocation with Lincoln and March engines coming north. Some of these were lodging turns, particularly in the case of the freight workings; thus, the 9p.m. Whitemoor-Ardsley via Boston would perhaps bring a V2 to lodge, returning on the 12.55a.m. Ardsley-Whitemoor next day. More impressive was the 8.40p.m. Whitemoor-Niddrie with a March V2 'lodger' which would tackle the 3.50p.m. Niddrie-York on the next day.

The Joint line thus saw much activity, with movement originating from unexpected places, such as the 9.07p.m. Dagenham Dock-Niddrie Class C or the 2.15a.m. Norwood-Doncaster parcels train. For certain of these, Gainsborough Lea Road was a booked halt for water. Add to all the above the regular movement of coal wagons to and from March, and the picture is complete.

There remain two further railways to record which made an impact on the transport scene in North Lincs., though the first was more of a damp squib than an explosion. The Lancashire, Derbyshire & East Coast Railway was a pretentious concern with ambitions originating far across the Pennines with a line of route across the Peak District, through Derbyshire and ending in a dock of its own at Sutton. On the Lincs. side the route followed that proposed by the Sutton & Willoughby Railway of 1886. The dock idea was of great interest to the LD & ECR and some 300 acres were set aside by the Trinity House for the purpose, which was not in fact fulfilled. The LD & EC Act of 1895 gave sanction for the final line and also permitted the merging of the proposed line east of Lincoln and the dock railways into the Lincoln & East Coast Railway and Dock Company of 1897, a project which died a natural death on the opening of Immingham Dock in 1906. However, a more modest LD & EC line opened in 1907, running from Chesterfield Market Place station. Now part of the GCR, it served six collieries and had a 59 arch viaduct at Fledborough with four girder sections in the length where it crossed the Trent. West of this point was High Marnham power station on the south side of the line, opened in 1962. This entered Lincs. shortly before Skellingthorpe station which lay just south of its village. Just over 1¼ miles further east the line ran into the Joint Line at Pyewipe Jc.

LD & EC interests east of Lincoln had of course been abandoned and there was left a truncated piece of route along which a squad of tank engines plodded. The signal boxes owed a lot to the GNR in appearance, while the most impressive station on the line was the junction at Langwith. Very few passenger trains ran before the end of things, as witness the workings in 1949 on Weekdays Only:

Departures from Lincoln Cen. at 9.35a.m., 12.45p.m., 3.37p.m. and 6.25p.m., arriving at Chesterfield Market Place at 11.24a.m., 2.33p.m., 5.30p.m. and

8.13p.m. The 3.37p.m. originated from Skegness and ran on Summer Saturdays Only.

In the other direction out of Chesterfield ran the 8.30a.m. express on Saturdays to Skegness, the 9.40a.m. and 4.10p.m., these arriving in Lincoln at 10.05a.m., 11.20a.m. and 5.52p.m. There was also a Skegness to Kirkby-in-Ashfield Saturdays Only working which called at Pyewipe Jc. for water at 3.22p.m. In the reverse direction a train left Leicester Cen. at 7.20a.m. on Summer Saturdays, calling at Lincoln at 9.44a.m. en route to Skegness.

Important freight workings used this line for part of its length to Clipstone Jc., via which they could gain Mansfield Concentration Sidings or the GC main line. The prime train of this genre was the No. 1 Braked Fish which left Grimsby Docks at 6.25p.m. with up to 45 vans, called for loco. purposes at Pyewipe Jc. and reached Banbury at 1 a.m. Empties would most likely return on a train out of Woodford at 4.15a.m. arriving at Grimsby at 2.15p.m. Latterly the line lost much of its importance and was singled in some places. A derailment in 1980 blocked one section of it and consideration was given to closure between the Trent crossing and Pyewipe Jc.

The other line was the Midland Railway branch from Nottingham via Newark which had arrived in Lincoln from an almost due south westerly direction, opened on 3rd August 1846. The MS & L operated across the main road level crossing to the station on the west side, the arrangements being supervised here by a circular cabin. The station, named in BR days after the St. Marks Church nearby, was of four tracks, offering two platforms beneath a two bay overall roof. The lines were joined at the ends by small turntables. On the south side was a small two road engine shed and turntable. The building on the north side suffered somewhat by being out of the sun and close to adjacent property, but had a fine portico of York stone on Classic lines which survived long after the turntables and the overall roof had gone. In true economical Midland manner the yard layout, all of which was of necessity west of the station, was supervised by two signal boxes of modest proportions, the Station cabin dealing with passenger train movements, and the West box which was of more importance, controlling, as well as a level crossing, the exit to eleven sidings, a timber yard and two engineering works on the south side, and five long sidings for goods and coal on the north side. On the same side beyond the crossing was a ground frame controlling movements to the Ruston & Hornsby factory. Within the Lincs. boundary there were stations at Hykeham, a not very ambitious site with staggered platforms and perhaps too near the city suburbs to have a character of its own, and Thorpe-on-the-hill which closed first on the line (7th February 1955). Swinderby station was set between two level crossings and with the village a mile away on the south side. Further away still on the far side of the A46 was the RAF base which generated quite an amount of traffic. The line was noted for the architecture of its stations, designed largely by I. A. Davies, and the best of these designs, as at Collingham, Newark Midland and Thurgarton, the latter in a gay Tudor style with riotous chimneys, lie outside the scope of this work.

The crossings in Lincoln had always created huge problems, and the two crossings of High Street remained long after the Pelham Street crossing had been dealt with, receiving electrified gates in 1925, then a bridge in 1958.

There had been early attempts to put in a spur from the Market Rasen direction to run east to the GN & GE Joint line, suggested in 1909 and 1924 to save traffic through Lincoln and reversals, but nothing came of the idea. In 1963 consideration was given to the closure of St. Marks station and the Newark line; instead the GN line running due south to Grantham was closed and the crossings remained. Two years later a plan was proposed to run a spur from the Midland line into Central from the west, thus closing St. Marks and its related crossing, This, too, foundered, as did a move to plan a new station combining both old ones, for which the city authorities refused to spend the £2000,000 required. Now of course the wheel has turned full circle, St. Marks is closed and all trains use Central.

Latterly St. Marks and the MR line actually grew in importance, and one of the prime reasons for this lay to the north where heavy freight workings such as the Barnetby High Dyke and Immingham-Colwick were running through Grimsby Town, causing problems at the level crossings there, before turning south towards Louth. In June 1964 a suggestion was made that a curve should be put in at Wrawby Jc. to bring eastbound iron-ore trains round to the Lincoln line to avoid either the plod through Grimsby or reversal at Barnetby. This project foundered because of the cost of £250,000, a pity as the idea was feasible using the land available. By this arrangement trains could have saved a detour via Grimsby and Louth, though only the original 1909 spur could have saved the Lincoln level crossings from the extra traffic. What transpired was the closure of the East Lincs. through route from Grimsby to Boston in 1970, and all the ore traffic and the rest was reversed at Barnetby and passed via Lincoln through St. Marks and over the Midland up to the flat crossing with the ECML at Newark. Here a connection had been put in during 1965 to bring the traffic southwards. Thus Louth lost its through service, Grimsby had less traffic over its level crossings, but Lincoln had more.

D11 No. 62664 at Grimsby in July 1950 ready to take a Kings Cross - Cleethorpes train over the final section. This train of eleven coaches would block the level crossings at both ends. *M. Black*

In 1980 there were only three regularly running loco. hauled passenger trains over this route, these being the King's Cross-Cleethorpes workings. In 1978 Class 55 'Deltic' locomotive Nos. 55005/12/22 could be found on the 8.25a.m. from King's Cross and 13.18 return, and the 13.04 outward and 17.31 return. One further loco. hauled working was the morning Grimsby-Manchester train.

J11 on local train at Lincoln Cen.   C. T. Goode

The Docks at Grimsby and Immingham have (in recent years) always played an important role in the commerce of the North Lincolnshire area and within the wider spectrum of the country as a whole. Both ports came into their own especially during the Second World War, and hitherto had concentrated on the handling of commodities as follows:

Immingham: Imports of pit props, timber and iron ore. Exports of coal, iron, steel and slag.

Grimsby: Imports of Danish butter, eggs, bacon, timber from the Baltic and Russia, seed potatoes from Scotland. Exports of fish.

In both ports the docks were requisitioned for military purposes in wartime Immingham was the HQ of the Humber Flag Officer. During the Great War Admiralty coal had been moved from South Wales to Immingham in up to nine trains per day, this arriving via Banbury and usually hauled by one of the 521 04 2-8-0 locomotives. The signalman at Ulceby Jc. must indeed have been busy at this time, especially when it was reckoned that some 5,500 special trains were also run for conveying troops!

During 1942-4 Immingham saw the Americans arrive to discharge their landing craft and army vehicles from the 'Victory' ships. Vessels were also loaded for Russia, the Gulf, North Africa and Normandy, to which latter place went the Mulberry piers which were marshalled at Immingham. As the continent was liberated, so the loading and despatch of shipping intensified, particularly to Antwerp.

Enemy action was light at Immingham during 1939-45, in fact Nazi fury was concentrated on Hull, where in two nights during May 1941 over 1,000 wagons were lost. During 1914-18 there were 59 air raid alerts in the area, with incendiary bombs on Grimsby, high explosive bombs at Halton and the death of a signalman at Immingham. In a Zeppelin raid on 31st January 1916 at Frodingham four staff were injured in the goods yard.

Things were more lively at Grimsby where, in 1939-45 there were 37 air raids, during which the fish market, No. 2 fish dock and warehouse were destroyed. Significant, too, was the reduction by the Admiralty of the 430 trawlers to 68. By the mid fifties this number had risen to about 300 working in and out of No. 1 fish dock for North Sea trawlers and No.2 fish dock for middle and deep water vessels, all served by road and rail. Negotiations were handled by some 500 fish merchants. The railway dealt in small loads of up to one ton in up to 300 vans daily with 40% rebate if merchants sent fish to one of eight specific centres and 25% if they used rail exclusively, as many opted for road in clement weather. The Ross factory already used only road haulage. As the traffic was somewhat hit and miss, odd vans were likely to appear on the rear of passenger trains to give that rare aroma as they breezed through country stations.

Considering the basic movements around 1955; empties were brought to New Clee from the 1.15a.m. ex King's Cross and 4a.m. Woodford. These were transferred by either J63 or J94 0-6-0 tanks to nine areas around the docks. Some loaded vans would find their way to passenger services such as the 11.29a.m. Sheffield, 11.43 Lincoln and 2.22p.m. Sheffield which took North and Mid-Wales fish. This practice soon died once dmus became pervasive. At this time there were block fish trains; the 1.04p.m. Banbury via the Waleswood Curve (near Woodhouse) loading up to 35 wagons, the 4.48p.m. to Nottingham Mid. with 16 vans behind a 4F 0-6-0, while finally there was the 5.13p.m. Ashton Moss (Manchester) via Retford. Latterly B1s and K3s covered the Eastern Region turns, sometimes double-headed. The 5.13p.m. working ran via Doncaster for many years, calling at Marshgate and booked through at 7.45p.m., usually with up to 45 vans on behind a B7 4-6-0 which really did let the neighbourhood know that it was on the move, a most impressive sight and sound.

London had two fish trains, the 5.30p.m. and 5.58p.m. which were eventually combined to form the 5.30p.m. worked up by a Boston crew with an Immingham K3 who returned on the empties at 1.15a.m. on weekdays and the 2.25a.m. Boston news on Sundays. There was also the 6.25p.m. Fish to Leicester via Tuxford.

As in many areas recession brought about cut-backs to the fishing industry in Grimsby and Hull, the latter in particular having become but a shadow of its former self, and rail traffic in the commodity has virtually ceased.

In later steam days was largely B1 or K3 types on excursions and the more unusual traffic. The Cleethorpes-Birmingham service had a B1, but failures of the class proved embarrassing when Saltley Class 5s were substituted, and on one memorable day, 4th September 1954 a Gloucester 4-4-0 No. 40930 took charge and ran through to Cleethorpes. Eason's, a local travel agent, organised excursions to the Capital for several years which were often Pacific hauled. In September 1948 such an excursion of a ten bogies was timed to leave Cleethorpes at 6.15a.m. and to return there at 4.23a.m., giving a good value day out to at least two groups travelling on the 11th., namely the Shire Trawlers party and the 200 members of the Tagcraft party joining at Boston.

To Immingham came the Orient Line Specials which always caused a Flurry at the Docks, with clamped points and flagmen in evidence. The Appendix stated:

'During the period from 20 minutes before the time of Arrival of the first Special and the Arrival of the second Special at Immingham Dock, and from 20 minutes before the booked time of departure of the first Special until after the second Special has cleared Immingham East Jc., no engine other than the Special train engines must be permitted to pass between the East Jc. and Transit Sheds or to foul the lines over which the Special trains will run.' As the trains are of particular interest, the following details of running are given for two occasions in July 1939, before they stopped for good:

Train No. 249. Conveys dining car stores Marylebone-Neasden Sidings arr. 9.20a.m.
Train No. 250. First Class Only. Ex Neasden Sidings 10.20a.m. Made up of ten coaches plus restaurant cars. Leaves Marylebone 11.48a.m. and calls Rugby, Leicester, Nottingham Vic., then runs via Tuxford. Calls at Pyewipe Jc. 3.31p.m. for water and arrives Immingham Dock East at 4.41p.m.
Train No. 251. Composite. Departs Neasden Sidings at 11.14a.m. Made up of seven coaches plus restaurant car. Leaves Marylebone at 12 noon and calls as above buts runs via Waleswood Curve and Retford to arrive Immingham at 4.54p.m.

Train No. 252. Composite. Light engine runs tender first from Ardwick to Manchester Cen. arrive 1.43p.m. Train leaves at 2.10p.m. made up of eight coaches plus restaurant and large parcels van which must be next to engine. Calls at Guide Bridge, Penistone and Sheffield Vic. at 3.32p.m. where a through carriage off the 1.18p.m. out of Liverpool Cen. is attached to rear. Then Retford at 4.11p.m. where a compo. brake from Glasgow is attached to the rear off the 10.15a.m. out of Edinburgh which halts for the purpose. Arrival at Immingham of this assemblage is 5.35p.m.

The return Specials left Immingham at 9.25a.m. for Marylebone (Nos. 253 and 254). Both ran via Waleswood, calling at the same stops en route and arriving at 2.48p.m. and 3.09p.m. respectively. The first away was the First Class Only train. In one evocative footnote No. 253 was to precede the 11.56a.m. steam railcar ex Basford & Bulwell at Bagthorpe Jc!

The Manchester Central train No. 255 left at 10.25 a.m., arriving at 1.48p.m. with the outward arrangements in reverse order. The Glasgow coach joined the 10.05a.m. ex King's Cross at Retford, and this time the Liverpool coach went through to Manchester and was transferred to the 2p.m. out. Crews went outward from Immingham, lodged and brought fresh trains 'home' the next day.

There were many fascinating excursions in July 1939; to go from Wigan to Scunthorpe on a regular special working might well be in order, but it was pushing matters somewhat to find a similar excursion running on the same days from Scunthorpe to Wigan and back. Possibly a sort of Mutual Commiseration Society. And what of the evening excursions from Cleethorpes to Skegness and back? These left at 4.15p.m. and 5.20p.m. getting back at 11.50p.m. and 11.48p.m., the coaching being described as 'having narrow seats for 1,000'!

Immingham continues to survive quite healthily as a port with good rail links, and on the closure of the old steam shed a new diesel depot was built to the south east of it which catered originally for 90 main line engines and 35 shunters. The building measured 367ft. x 79ft. and was double ended with a central stores and admin. section flanked by a maintenance section at one end and service section at the other. Here 'foreign' locomotives could be inspected as required.

The position at New Holland has been radically changed since the opening of the Humber Bridge in June 1981 and the rail emphasis has shifted to an hourly service between Cleethorpes and Barton, serving New Holland and linking up at the latter place with the National bus service 350 between Hull and Scunthorpe. In some respects, depending on where one wishes to go, the service has never been better. Four trips are run to Brigg by Cross Coaches from Barton, but anyone trying to get from the Barton area to Gainsborough by public transport is in for a nasty shock.

New Holland Pier and P.S. Grimsby.   *Hull Libraries*

Humber Ferry - P.S. Killingholme at the opening of Immingham Dock, 1912.

Hull Libraries

The decline and end of the Humber ferry has been adequately recorded elsewhere, so that due reference here might be less tediously done by concentrating on the economic reasons for closure. In 1979 there were ten sailings in each direction, nearly all of which gave rail connection to or from Grimsby and Barton. There was one less on Sundays. The normal return for an adult was £1.08 and for a normal car £5.40. At this time one vessel, the diesel electric 'Faringford' built in 1947 ran the service, capable of taking 500 passengers and 36 vehicles. Should the vessel have broken down, a light pleasure steamer the 'Yorkshire Belle' was available from Bridlington, capable of taking 208 foot passengers in summer and 146 in winter. In 1978 the following were carried:

Foot passengers:	to Hull 220,731.	from Hull: 222,007.
Motorists:	to Hull 86,620.	from Hull: 87,899
Cars:	to Hull 37,874.	from Hull: 38,225.

Receipts for the ferry workings were:

	1976	1977	1978
Gross:	£490,000	£509,000	£518,000
Expenses:	£551	£719	£542,000

Consideration was given to various options to keep some sort of ferry running. A new vessel would cost £2 million, a passenger only vessel £½ million and the continued loan of 'Yorkshire Belle' £5,000 per annum, plus daily hire charges. Sealink owned New Holland pier and they estimated that annual maintenance costs there would be £100,000, a similar though slightly less figure being quoted by Hull Corporation for their pontoon.

New Holland Pier showing GC signals still in situ and Hull ferry in background.
R. F. Mitchell

87

Unbelievable, but this was the normal view each morning as workmen left the ferry for New Holland.

During a sample week's survey of ferry usage, investigators found a total of 13,330 passengers with a high level of commuting/business journeys on a regular basis. Of those travelling to Hull, the majority were heading for work in the city centre with most of these from Brigg. Of 98 passengers heading from north to south the majority came from Hull proper and most were bound for places of work in Scunthorpe (25), Killingholme (18), Immingham (11), Grimsby (16) and New Holland (5).

The new bridge, regarded as an expensive luxury by some, is convenient and accepted locally, the only disadvantages being the toll charges and enforced closure in high winds. 'Lincoln Castle' is, at the time of writing, set in permanent moorings high and dry on the Hessle shore and used as a restaurant. The 'Faringford' is awaiting a decision on her fate which will possibly mean her eventual transfer to ferry work in Western Scotland.

Mention must be made of the only privately owned passenger carrying railway in North Lincolnshire, the Lincolnshire Coast Light Railway run by an Association of the same name. The line was laid adjacent to the holiday area south of Cleethorpes called Humberstone Fittes in 1960, using ex WD 60cm. track from the Nocton Estates Light Railway, with metal sleepers. The layout was completed using cut-down standard gauge sleepers and ex Penrhyn flat bottom rail laid to the 2 foot gauge along a straight run with a little covered over terminus, office and authentic signals at the west end. After weathering legal problems due to an accident on the lone, a service of trains was resumed during late 1981. At the time when these notes were compiled there were four locomotives available:

No.1 'Nocton' a 4 wheel Motor rail Simplex of 1926.

No.2 'Southam' a 4 wheel Ruston & Hornsby of 1933.

No.3 'Jurassic' a Peckett 0-6-0 of 1903.

No.4 'Wilton' a 4 wheel Motor rail Simplex of 1940.

Interested readers may find other books by the same author of use:-
"Railways in East Yorkshire"   (Oakwood Press)
"Midland Railway-Derby-Lincoln"   (C. T. Goode)

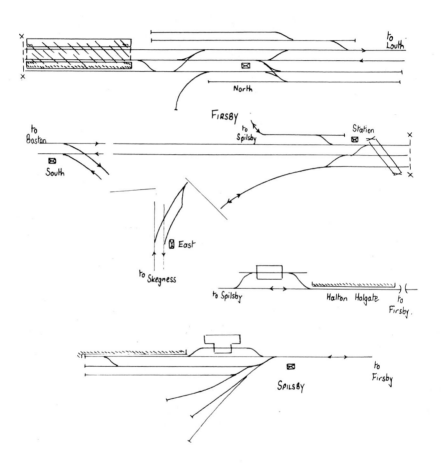

to
Louth

North

FIRSBY

to
Boston

South

to
Spilsby

Station

East

to Skegness

to Spilsby

Halton Holgate

to
Firsby.

SPILSBY

to
Firsby

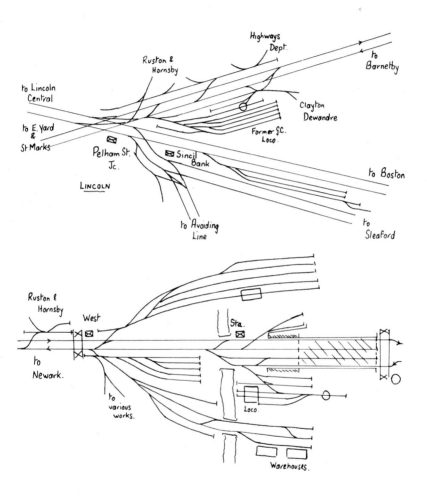

to Barnetby

Highways
Dept.

Ruston &
Hornsby

to Lincoln
Central

Clayton
Dewandre

to E. Yard
&
St Marks

Former G.C.
Loco.

Pelham St.
Jc.

Sincil
Bank

to Boston

LINCOLN

to Avoiding
Line

to
Sleaford

Ruston &
Hornsby

West

Sta.

to
Newark.

to
various
works.

Loco.

Warehouses.

91

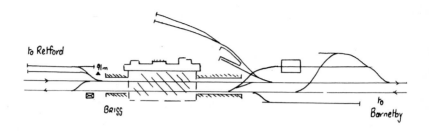

to Retford

91m

Briss

to Barnetby

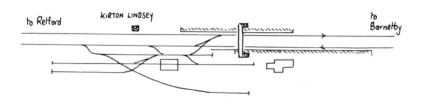

to Retford

KIRTON LINDSEY

to Barnetby

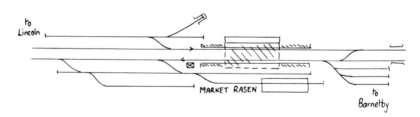

to Lincoln

MARKET RASEN

to Barnetby

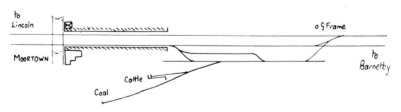

to Lincoln

o G Frame

MOORTOWN

Cattle

Coal

to Barnetby

2

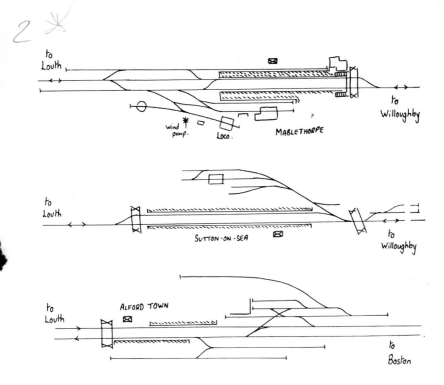

to
Louth

to
Willoughby

Wind
pump.

Loco.

MABLETHORPE

to
Louth

SUTTON-ON-SEA

to
Willoughby

ALFORD TOWN

to
Louth

to
Boston

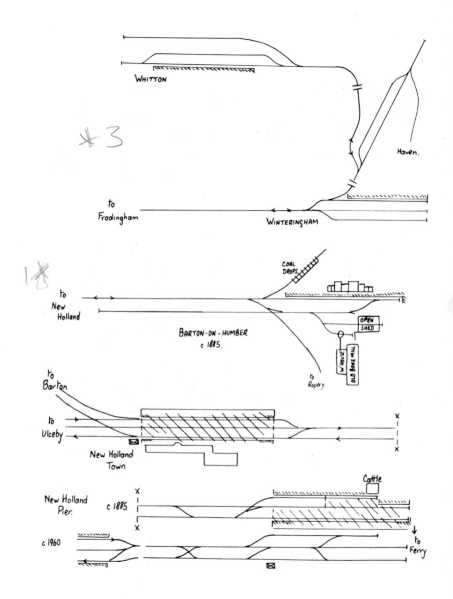

WHITTON

✳ 3

Haven.

to
Frodingham

WINTERINGHAM

COAL
DROPS.

to
New
Holland

OPEN
SHED

BARTON-ON-HUMBER
c 1885.

W. HOUSE

OLD BONE MILL

to
Ropery

to
Barton

to
Ulceby

New Holland
Town

New Holland
Pier.

c 1885.

Cattle

c 1960

to
Ferry

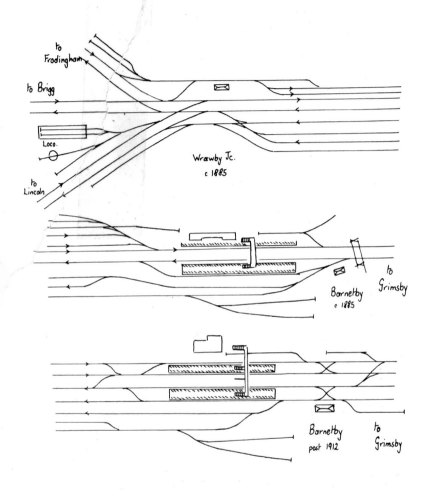

to
Frodingham

to Brigg

Loco.

to
Lincoln

Wrawby Jc.
c 1885

Barnetby
c 1885

to
Grimsby

Barnetby
post 1912

to
Grimsby

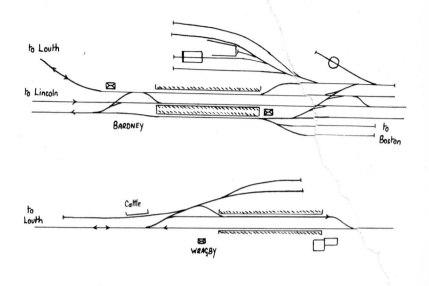

to Louth

to Lincoln

BARDNEY

to
Boston

Cattle

to
Louth

WRAGBY

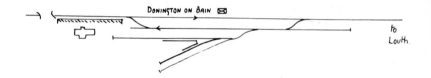

DONINGTON ON BAIN

to
Louth.

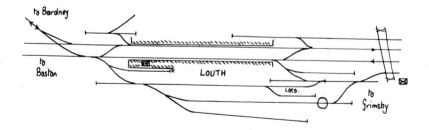

to Bardney

to
Boston

LOUTH

Loco.

to
Grimsby

96

Designed & Printed by Swannack, Brown & Co. Ltd., 13a Anlaby Road, Hull.